D0682378

HOW IT ALL BEGAN IN THE GARDEN

HOW IT ALL BEGAN IN THE GARDEN

The Stories Behind Common or Garden Names

MAURICE BAREN

Smith
Settle

First published in 1994 by

Smith Settle Ltd
Ilkley Road
Otley
West Yorkshire
LS21 3JP

© Maurice Baren 1994

All rights reserved. No part of this book may be reproduced, stored or introduced into a retrieval system, or transmitted in any form or by any means (electronic, mechanical, photocopying, recording or otherwise) without the permission of Smith Settle Ltd.

The right of Maurice Baren to be identified as the author of this work has been asserted by him in accordance with the Copyright, Designs and Patents Act 1988.

ISBN Paperback   1 85825 022 6
      Hardback   1 85825 023 4

British Library Cataloguing-in-Publication Data:
A catalogue record is available for this book from the British Library.

Designed, printed and bound by
SMITH SETTLE
Ilkley Road, Otley, West Yorkshire LS21 3JP

This book is dedicated firstly to my father, the late Wilfred Baren, who was a nurseryman, and gave me my first love of gardening and encouraged me so much in my career and life among plants.

Also to Ken Wilson under whom I first worked at Ilkley Parks nursery, and to the late 'P K' Willmott, for many years head of horticulture at Askham Bryan College, York, who helped so many young people find their way in horticulture.

I owe them so much.

Pictorial acknowledgements

A-Z Botanical Library, p63; Judith Baren, p45; Jelena de Belder, p51*(m)*; Robert Bolton & Son, p70; Sarah Bowen, p9*(b)*; Burpee Seeds, p104*(l)*; Canadian Post Office, p24*(b)*; East Malling Research Station, p26*(b)*; Terence E Exley, pp4, 6*(b)*, 32, 54*(b)*, 55*(t)*, 60*(t)*, 79*(r)*, 83*(t)*, 84*(t)*, 91*(b)*, 120*(tl)*; Dr & Mrs J Farrer, pp85, 87; Flymo Ltd, pp112, 113; R Fulger, pp21, 25; Harkness Roses, p47*(b)*; Peter Harkness, pp39, 40*(r)*, 42*(t)*, 47*(t)*; Tom Hewitt, p14; Mrs E M Hill, p13; Robert Hillier, pp97*(b)*, 98, 99; John Innes Horticultural Institute, p107; Michael Johnson, p22*(b)*; Joyce Kidd, p105; Bridget Lendrum, p19*(l)*; David Mycock, xi; Potato Marketing Board, p75; RBG, Edinburgh, pp58, 62*(t)*, 86, 89*(t)*; RHS Lindley Library, pp3, 8*(b)*, 12*(t)*, 15*(t)*, 42, 52*(t)*, 67*(b)*, 72, 73*(t)*, 90*(b)*, 96*(t)*, and pp23 & 29 from *Hooker's Finest Fruits*; Chris G Rose, pp8*(t)*, 36, 51*(b)*, 52*(b)*, 89*(b)*, 90*(t)*, 121; Shropshire Local Studies Library, p66*(b)*; Slough Borough Council, p72*(t)*; Harry Smith Horticultural Photographic Library, pp27*(t)*, 46, 49*(l)*, 53*(l)*, 59, 82, 107*(l)*; Earl Spencer, p68; Celia Steven, p17; Suffolk Record Office, pp27*(b)*, 29; Suttons Seeds, p101*(b)*; Frank Toynbee, p11*(b)*; M Tyerman, p93*(b)*; Wendy Walsh, p65; J F Woolman, p92; University of Liverpool, p103*(l)*.

Contents

Foreword by Geoffrey Smith

'All that is worth remembering in life is the poetry of it', according to William Hazlitt. Certainly, those gardeners who are satisfied with the simple routine of burying the brown end in the soil, then sitting back to wait for the flowers to appear, miss so much of the romance and lyric quality of gardening.

What's in a name? In most cases a potted history of the plant which it identifies. Russell lupins, Shirley poppies and Ballard michaelmas daisies are a part of the romantic history of gardening.

Possibly it is apples which excite the imagination. Who sowed the pips which produced a Cox's Orange Pippin, and who for that matter was Mr Cox or, indeed, the Mr or Mrs Bramley who gifted pomologists with Bramley's seedlings? These are just one or two of those fascinating garden mysteries amongst the many this book solves.

No gardener worthy of the name is ever satisfied with a plant as it is, for if they were, instead of the splendid hybrid tea and floribunda roses, we would still be cultivating the single-flowered wild species. *How It All Began in the Garden* describes how in some families, sons and grandsons have carried on the work of producing new improved varieties of roses begun seventy or more years ago.

A great deal of painstaking research has gone into the writing of this book: a meticulous gleaning of facts and not just from dusty volumes tucked away in reference libraries. Some of the most stimulating pen sketches have come from personal interviews, first-hand information not previously recorded.

Each page opens a window on gardening, offering a view which invites further exploration. What could have been a historical record, dry with the dust of endless years, is, in fact, a very readable, conversational book which delivers hard facts in a way which fixes them firmly in the memory. After all if, as Lord Bacon asserted, 'gardening is the greatest refreshment to the spirits of man', then discovering the richness of the legacy bequeathed to us by previous generations of horticulturalists through reading about them, must be the best possible relaxation of the mind of man.

Maurice Baren is well-qualified both in horticultural and academic terms to write a book which combines the romance of gardening with proven historical fact. That he has spent over fifteen years accumulating and checking the correctness of the facts contained in this work is a tribute to his dedication and interest in the subject.

Geoffrey Smith   Harrogate   1994

Author's note

This book has been 'growing' for over fifteen years, and during that period many people have kindly given me pieces of information or recommended where I could find a particular 'history' or story — to all I am most grateful. Information, in some cases, has come from more than one source, in some instances long before the idea of a book appeared possible, and if you feel that I have not acknowledged your help I do apologise.

However, I would particularly like to thank the following for their help: Lord Aberconway, Atco Ltd, Harold Baker, Peter Barnes, Jelena de Belder, Sarah Bowen, Rev Fr Killan Brennan, Chris Brickell, Jenny Bryan, W Atlee Burpee Co, Jim Deen, Graham Dixon, Dr and Mrs J Farrer, Jack Harkness, Peter Harkness, Haws Ltd, Robert Hillier, Tom and Peggy Hewitt, Mrs Hill, John Innes Institute, Michael Johnson, Dr Fred Kidd, Bridget Lendrum, Richard Moore, National Trust, Dr Charles Nelson, Brigid Noctor, Ransomes Ltd, Audrey Robinson, Lynn Robson (Flymo), Louis R Russell, Keith Sangster, Tony Schilling, Bill Simpson, Ken Smith, Earl Spencer, Celia Steven, Suttons Seeds, A D Todhunter, Margaret Tyerman, JF Woolman.

I would also like to acknowledge the help given by the following library and archive services: Berkshire County Council, City of Bradford Central Library, Derbyshire County Council, Devon County Council, Hereford & Worcester County Council, Institute of Horticultural Research, University of Liverpool, Nottinghamshire County Council, Royal Botanic Gardens of Kew and Edinburgh, Stevenage Museum, York City Library, and particularly the librarians and staff of the Lindley Library of the Royal Horticultural Society who have been so helpful. Special thanks are extended to all the staff at Smith Settle Ltd for their help and friendliness. Once again the support of my wife, Judith, has been tremendous and is much appreciated.

My task would have been impossible but for the records contained within horticultural magazines and journals — to the editors of such magazines and journals of our current generation, I plead that they also include modern elements of what to future generations will be 'horticultural social history'.

Have you ever wondered who Granny Smith was, of apple fame of course? Or what about John Innes, or do we only know of his compost? Down the garden path we meet numerous people who are familiar to us as plant names, but what do we know of them as people, real people?

In this book I have attempted to bring to life our friends, normally known to us as flowers, fruit or familiar products, showing something of them as men and women. Of course some plants are associated with the place where they were found, or with the person who found them; some have been developed in famous gardens; others in the most unusual places. Never have so many of these different backgrounds been brought together in one book, but I am most grateful for those who, in years past, have written down perhaps even one such story, for without their lead this work would not have been possible. Some of the material has never been published before and I hope this work will contribute to the social history of gardening.

How It All Began in the Garden includes such famous names as Russell (and his lupins), Ena Harkness (and her rose), Cox (of the 'Orange Pippin') and Logan (and his berry). Have you ever grown the French marigold 'Naughty Marietta'? But why 'Naughty Marietta'? The answer's here! Have you ever wondered what the first lawnmower looked like, or who invented it? The story is here. John Innes never knew the value of his compost or of the way it would revolutionise the growing of plants. Why not? You'll have to find the answer in the book!

Like its companion *How It All Began*, the story of some of our most famous household brand names, this book not only tells a story, a fascinating story, but all the way through it is generously illustrated in colour and black and white.

It is a ready reference book to answer your unusual questions. It is a dipping-in book to have at the side of the bed or by your favourite chair; it will also make a much appreciated gift for a young or more elderly person.

This work is the culmination of over fifteen years' research, of dead ends, of frustrations and disappointment, but also of surprise, amusement and even joy!

On Christopher Wren's tomb, in St Pauls Cathedral, are inscribed the words: 'If you seek his memorial, look around you'. Surely this applies to the men and women who have brought us our plants, and thereby have enriched our lives.

'If you have two pennies, spend one for a loaf and one for a flower.
The bread will give you life; the flower a reason for living.'
Chinese proverb

Maurice E Baren
Haworth   1994

George Russell, a man with an eye for the right plant, and **(right)** some of the lupins he produced.

1.
Wanderings in the Flower Garden

The landscape architects may love their shades of green, or the beauty of texture and form, but, to many British gardeners, colour and beauty of flowers are of prime importance.

George Russell obviously had a great love of colour, but wanted much more from the lupins he worked so hard to improve.

He was born at Stillington, about ten miles north of York in 1857, the fifth child of a master shoemaker, John Russell and his wife Susan. When he grew up he started work as a jobbing gardener in York, and one of the houses where he worked was on the Mount. It was there, in the home of Mrs Micklethwaite, that he saw a vase of lupins and felt that they could be, and should be, improved. Up to the early part of this century, the lupin was a poor plant with flowers widely placed on the stem and with a restricted colour range — shades of blue, white and pale pink.

It was not until 1911, when he was over fifty years old, that Russell started his work on lupins, and this work was to fill the remainder of his life.

He commenced his developments with *Lupinus polyphyllus*, a Canadian species introduced by David Douglas, but eventually used many other species. He had no nursery, only an allotment on Bishopthorpe Road. He knew nothing of Mendel's laws of heredity, but had an eye for the right plant when it came along, and limitless patience. His selection process was simple, but severe: he kept only those he liked best. He destroyed all the others before they could adversely affect the next generation of seedlings.

It was not long before he needed a second allotment and soon both were filled with lupin seedlings. By 1925 his allotments had become a showpiece when the lupins were in flower, and many people wanted to buy a plant, but always the answer was 'No'.

Until a certain man came along! Mr James Baker was a nurseryman from Codsall, near Wolverhampton, and he approached Russell in a different way. He too was a lupin fanatic and had already visited a nursery at Leeming Bar in Yorkshire (probably that of Messrs Harkness, related to the famous rose growers now based at Hitchin, but who in those days were raisers of new lupins). There Baker had seen between 8 and 10 acres of lupins.

At Leeming Bar he had chosen only one plant, but on seeing the lupins of

George Russell he exclaimed: 'In all my lifelong career I have never seen such an astonishing and unforgettable sight. As to the flames and the salmons, they simply took my breath away'.

Mr Baker was himself seventy-four years old, an experienced plantsman and a shrewd judge. We are told that the conversation went as follows. Mr Baker opened with: 'You are being selfish, you are keeping all this beauty to yourself instead of sharing it with other people who love flowers'. The old man came back: 'They can come and look'; but he was, for the first time, on the defensive. 'You're nearly eighty', said Mr Baker, 'What's going to happen when you die? Your flowers will die with you and be lost to the world.'

'I've seen to that', said George Russell, 'I've trained the boy to my ways. He'll have them when I die and he can go on'. The boy was Sonny Heard who, when a child, had contracted a form of paralysis. The doctors had given up hope, but not so George Russell. He had carried the lad on his back.

4

Russell lupins

Once again Mr Baker took up the attack: 'You get up at four and five in the morning to see that nobody steals your plants, but the boy won't be able to.' At last Russell gave in, but not immediately. Mr Baker went back home and it was only after three sleepless nights that George Russell 'wired' Codsall saying 'Yes'. He sold every plant on his allotments. Mr Baker tried to persuade him to keep a few, but George Russell replied: 'You've paid for them. You're going to put them on the market as Russell lupins. It would not be right for me to go on growing them.'

In an hour or two his allotments were empty and twenty years of his life had gone with the plants. However, one condition he had insisted on: the boy must go with the lupins, so the lad's future was secure.

The next year, 1936, he went to Codsall to do the 'selecting' of the plants and Mr Baker and his staff must have looked on in alarm as they watched George Russell and Sonny throw out hundreds of plants. From a total of 5,000 plants they left only 800 — the rest did not meet their standards!

'With a veritable blaze of rich and exotic colour, the Russell Lupin literally burst upon an astonished gardening world on a June day in 1937'. So wrote Ronald Parrett in the opening words of his book, *The Russell Lupins*. The first seed and seedlings of Russell lupins were offered to the public in January 1938 by Baker's Nurseries Ltd. Thirty-one different named varieties were for sale in that first year and several of these were still available over twenty years later. These included 'Mrs Micklethwaite', salmon; 'City of York', flame-red; 'George Russell', pale coral pink, with creamy white, pink-edged standards; and 'Mrs Noel Terry', pale-blush pink bells and creamy-white standards (the latter were named because Russell's allotments were behind Terry's chocolate factory, land now used as a municipal carpark for the racecourse).

At the first fortnightly show of the Royal Horticultural Society, following the Chelsea Flower Show, the *Gardeners' Chronicle* reported: 'On a considerable wall space Messrs Bakers Ltd displayed a magnificent collection of the Russell lupins. These lovely varieties represent twenty years' work by a little-known gardener, who has produced strains of surpassing excellence, which are characterised by dwarf, sturdy habit and long, erect spikes of many lovely colours. The pinks and rose-coloured varieties predominate, but Mr Russell evidently also has a fancy for the bicolours, of which here were many clearly marked sorts. We understand seeds of his outstanding type will be available next year.'

George Russell was awarded the Veitch Memorial Medal by the Royal Horticultural Society for his outstanding work, which he had started at the age of fifty-five; now he was eighty-one years old. He lived on to the age of ninety-four, among his plants at Boningdale. He, alone, knew their secrets.

There are many English clergymen who have made a major contribution to our gardens and the Rev Henry Harpur Crewe was one of them. He was born in

ILLUSTRATED

18

Add Distinction to your garden

GLORIOUS FLOWERS
AT LITTLE COST!

Bishop DELPHINIUMS

This unique strain, rich in intense true blues, the like of which have never before been seen in Delphiniums, and many other delightful shades, together with the large individual florets and perfectly-balanced spikes, put Bishop Delphiniums in a class by themselves.

2/6, 5/-, 10/-, 20/- pkt., post free,
with raisers' full cultural instructions.

Russell Lupins

The genuine Re-selected Stock distributed in packets bearing a photograph of Mr. George Russell is the finest strain in cultivation. It has been slowly built up year after year on our re-selection.

Brilliant new reds, rich yellows, in addition to lovely pinks and many other shades, on massive spikes characteristic of the best Russell type.

Latest re-selected stock.

2/6, 5/-, 10/- pkt., post free,
with raisers' full cultural instructions.

HERBACEOUS BORDERS

We are always ready to prepare plans free of cost, showing what we consider the most effective arrangement, and if you decide to take advantage of this service, the following information should be supplied :—

Dimensions and aspect of the border, indicating any section in the shade or partial shade.

DEPT. 13, CODSALL, WOLVERHAMPTON
England's Leading Hardy Plant Specialists

Cheiranthus 'Harpur Crewe'

The coat of arms of the Harpur Crewe family of Calke Abbey.

1830, and from 1860 he was rector of Drayton Beauchamp in Buckinghamshire.

He was an enthusiastic collector and cultivator of hardy plants, especially bulbs, and was a member of the Royal Horticultural Society's council. Sir Joseph D Hooker, in 1875, described his collection of crocuses as the 'richest in Europe'. The *Crocus crewei*, which was discovered by H G Elwes, was sent to Harpur Crewe. It was Elwes' request that it be called after the rector.

Many readers will know the small double yellow wallflower, known as *Cheiranthus* 'Harpur Crewe'. It has a long flowering season, and, like *C* 'Bowles Mauve', is ideal for the rock garden. How Rev Harpur Crewe obtained the wallflower is not known, but like most good gardeners he loved to share his treasures, and it is thought that one of his numerous friends who received one simply called it 'Harpur Crewe's Wallflower'. It received an award of merit in 1896, and the same year, when Messrs Paul put it into commerce, they called it *Cheiranthus* 'Harpur Crewe'.

Another clergyman who served horticulture well was the Rev William Wilks, who in 1866 became curate of the parish church at Shirley, near Croydon, and was appointed vicar in 1879, a post he held until his retirement in 1912 following cancer of the larynx.

In 1888 he became honorary secretary of the Royal Horticultural Society at a period when the society was at a particularly low ebb, the membership being a mere 1,108! During the period of his office the membership grew to almost 16,000, and the society replaced its hired rooms with a magnificent hall and offices, wholly free of debt, and changed its grounds at Chiswick for the new

Harpur Crewe's wallflower, a gem for the small border.

6

Shirley poppies remind us of Rev William Wilks, a great servant of the Royal Horticultural Society.

garden at Wisley. These were achievements to be proud of, but in addition he also gave us a beautiful plant.

He found a plant of *Papaver rhoeas* growing in a waste corner of his garden, next to some fields. This plant had flowers which had a narrow white edging to its four petals. The plant was carefully marked, and its seed was later saved and sown.

The following year, out of the 200 plants which grew, only four or five had flowers which were all edged white. The best of these were also marked, and again the seed was saved. The vicar followed this pattern for several years, and gradually the infusion of white grew larger, toning down the red and arriving at a pale pink, with one plant which was pure white — with the exception of the black blotch at the base of the petals.

Up to this point the black blotch was found in all the flowers, then suddenly it disappeared from one plant. Not gradually as happened with the tones in the upper portions of the flowers. It just disappeared completely, leaving a white blotch in its place. During the next thirteen years, or thereabouts, the black colour was completely eliminated from the whole race and subsequently no 'black rogues' appeared.

Unfortunately normal trade selection is not always so rigorous as that carried out by Rev. Wilks and some black blotched ones have recurred. It is interesting that the strain was obtained by simple selection without any other species being involved. The name 'Shirley Poppy' relates to that district of Croydon where he was vicar.

On his retirement in 1920, Wilks was elected a member of the council of the Royal Horticultural Society; today he is memorialised in the wrought-iron gates at the main entrance to the gardens at Wisley. He died suddenly in 1923.

His obituary, in the society's *Journal*, summed him up in these words: 'When in one man wisdom is added to knowledge, tact to firm handling of affairs, patience to tenacity of purpose, singleness of aim to ability, knowledge of man to love of nature and simple natural things, the cause to which that man attaches himself is bound to be well served.' Such a man was the Rev William Wilks!

In about 1905 Amos Perry, the famous nurseryman, sold two boxes of *Geum* to a Mr Bradshaw of the Grange, Southgate, now part of Enfield, on the edge of London. His gardener selected the double red-flowered type and it was named after Mrs Bradshaw. She, in her obituary in the local paper, is described as a reserved and somewhat austere woman, but who was kindness itself when she knew you. She was a great lover of flowers, and her beautiful garden at the

'Ada Ballard', named to commemorate Ernest Ballard's sister.

Ernest Ballard, the raiser of many of our modern Michaelmas daisies **(below and opposite)**.

Grange provided much brightness for the rooms of the sick and elderly. Mr John Bradshaw goes down in history for his railway timetables, and her gardener, Mr G G Whitelegg, for his famous rock gardens at Chelsea Show.

Geum 'Mrs Bradshaw' was introduced in 1931 by Messrs G & A Clark of Dover, a company established in 1838, and which, in 1929, employed nearly 300 people on nurseries extending to almost 250 acres. At that time they were selling about one million plants a year, in over 10,000 varieties.

It often seems that a plantsman cum nurseryman is not really interested in business, but in getting on with the job of growing or hybridising plants.

Ernest Ballard was such a man. He was born on the 2nd May 1871, the youngest of eight children of Stephen and Maria Ballard of Colwall. His father was a railway contractor and engineer, and therefore able to pay for Ernest to be educated first at a private school, followed by Malvern College, and later Birmingham University, where he obtained a degree in analytical chemistry.

For a time he helped with the large family estate before setting up with his brother Stephen in running a small malt vinegar factory in Colwall. This was not successful and in 1908 they dissolved the partnership: each went his separate way, Ernest entering a period of semi-retirement back at the Court in Colwall.

The garden there contained many gems, and Ernest, who had always been a keen hybridist and botanist, spent his days working amongst the plants. He raised the first double-flowered Michaelmas daisy and named it 'Beauty of Colwall': it

One of Whitelegg's famous rock gardens at the Chelsea Flower Show.

was awarded a first class certificate by the Royal Horticultural Society.

He was a short and sturdy man with a meticulous eye for a good plant. In a field of buttercups he happily exercised his extensive patience searching for variance of form or colour, where others less discerning would fail to see it. So it was that he has bequeathed us a wealth of cultivated plants — including over fifty varieties of Michaelmas daisy.

Only the best would bear the name of Colwall or Ballard — 'Ada Ballard' was his sister, 'Blandie' and 'Marie Ballard' are named after his second wife, 'Peggy Ballard' (raised as early as 1909) after his daughter, whilst later ones were named 'Helen' after his daughter-in-law, and 'Sarah' after his grand-daughter.

At the end of the war a famous trio of Michaelmas daisies was introduced — 'Peace', 'Plenty' and 'Prosperity' — a sign of hope for the years to come! Two other postwar varieties have stayed the course of time — 'Red Sunset' and 'Eventide'.

Ernest Ballard was a man of conflicting interests and ideas. He enjoyed shooting, both with a camera and a gun — and yet he hated cruelty. He came from a strong Nonconformist background, yet rarely went to church, and he married Marie who was a retired missionary.

He died in 1952, but not before the Royal Horticultural Society had awarded him its Victoria Medal for Horticulture.

A particularly attractive strain of the candelabra primula, *P japonica*, was developed over many years by Mr Dalrymple, who lived near the village of Bartley. The strain became *Primula japonica* 'Bartley Strain', after this small place, just off the Southampton to Ringwood road, on the edge of the New Forest. It is ideally suited to growing on a banking beside water.

The next plant will give you a banking of delightful bright-blue on the rock garden. Mr R H Macaulay, who had a wonderful garden at Kirnam, in Argyllshire, has been described as a scholar, athlete, East India merchant and gardener. He may have been all these, but many of us are just grateful that he gave us *Gentiana x macaulayi*, which is a cross between *G sino-ornata* and *G farreri*.

Not a true blue, more a lavender blue, is the giant catmint, *Nepeta* 'Six Hills

PLANT NOW

The Bartley Strain of
Primula pulverulenta

Lady Thursby, A.M., R.H.S., 1924. The best and most popular form. A beautiful shade of rose pink with yellow eye. **3/- each. 33/- dozen.**

Hew Dalrymple. A soft pink with a deep crimson eye, which makes a strong contrast. **1/6 each. 15/- dozen.**

Bartley Blush. A very pale blush pink, almost white, with yellow eye. **1/6 each. 15/- dozen.**

Bartley Pink. Soft pink with yellow eye. **1/6 each. 15/- per dozen.**

Bartley Strain, mixed. This contains Seedlings of all shades of pink, from blush to rose. **12/- doz. £4 15 0 per 100.**

Strong flowering plants for immediate delivery.

G. H. DALRYMPLE,
The Nurseries, Bartley,
nr. SOUTHAMPTON
Phone: Cadnam 23.

Above: *Candelabra primula* are ideal for growing in waterside areas.

Opposite Page Above: Clarence Elliott's nursery and the famous catmint were named after Stevenage's historic 'tumuli'.

Opposite Page Below: Frank Toynbee, whose home was called Croftway.

Giant'. The Six Hills Nursery belonged to Clarence Elliott and took its name from the six curious tumuli, Roman barrows which house cremated remains. The *Gardeners' Chronicle* of 1911 described it as adjoining 'the Great North Road on the south of the picturesque village of Stevenage, which chiefly consists of one long broad street, flanked by houses of various styles and dates'. How it has changed!

Clarence Elliott attended Giggleswick School, not far from Reginald Farrer's home at Clapham, but much preferred rambling to studies. However the science master, Dr Marshall Watts, instilled in him a love of botany. After leaving school he went to work for Messrs T S Rivers & Son at their nursery at Sawbridgeworth before moving to Backhouse's famous nursery at York. Here he worked in the alpine and herbaceous department, but soon the roaming instinct won and he started his travels, some with Reginald Farrer.

Clarence Elliott travelled far and near in search of rare plants, from the Falkland Islands, to the Austrian Alps. From Corsica he collected *Morisia hypogea*, a beautiful miniature alpine with yellow flowers, to gain a stronger strain. In 1928 in Patagonia he collected *Calceolaria darwinii*, and reintroduced them into cultivation. *Saxifraga primuloides* 'Elliott's Variety' was a form of this species which he collected near Lac d'Oo in the Pyrenees in 1911. In his own book *Rock Garden Plants*, published in 1935, he tells how he found this miniature London Pride, with its pale pink flowers: 'I was held up by a large and very cross bull, and I discovered my special *Saxifraga primuloides*. I felt that the common pink type left room for improvement, so I hunted — after eluding the bull — over several acres of the plant, hoping to find some variation from type, a form perhaps with guts. In the end I found it. A single plant, rather dwarfer than normal, with sprays of flowers of a clear, warm, deep pink, I collected a few rosettes, pleased, but little realising the importance of my discovery . . . The plant has gone into rock gardens in every corner of Europe, in Canada, New Zealand, Patagonia in fact in every temperate climate where folk garden.'

Before we move away from the Pyrenees let us consider just one more blue flower, again for the rock garden, native to these mountains, but its discoverer unknown. It was first found in cultivation in the garden of Dr Lowe who lived at Balgreen in Edinburgh and later at Woodcote near Wimbledon. As so often happens in gardening, one enthusiast tells another of a 'special plant' but also gives his friend a cutting or a young plant.

ALPINE SEEDS

Also Seeds of Choice Herbaceous, and the Cream of Annuals for cutting.

Interesting Catalogue sent by return on receipt of post card.

Clarence Elliott Ltd.
SIX HILLS NURSERY
STEVENAGE, HERTS.

Please mention THE GARDEN *when writing.*

In this case it was given to that great gardener E A Bowles, and from him to that equally famous plantsman and nurseryman, Amos Perry of Enfield, who introduced it to the public. The 'special plant' in this case was *Lithospermum prostratum* 'Heavenly Blue', now named *Lithodora diffusa* 'Heavenly Blue'. It is a lime hater and can be temperamental, but is well worth persevering with.

One worthwhile thing to come out of the First World War was, for Frank Toynbee, a government small-holding. It extended to about nineteen acres and on it he grew soft fruit. As house-building commenced on the new estates near Worthing, so he carried out the landscaping of their gardens. The name Croftway Nurseries was taken from the name of his home 'Croftway'.

The attractive herbaceous plant *Monarda* 'Croftway Pink' was raised at the nurseries in the mid 1930s, when Ken Aslett was nursery manager — he was later to become well known to garden lovers as the rock garden foreman at the Royal Horticultural Society's garden at Wisley. Other plants raised, or introduced, at the nurseries were *Sidalcea* 'Croftway Pink' and 'Croftway Red', and also *Gaillardia* 'Croftway Yellow'.

Still along the herbaceous border we are likely to come across an attractive and compact white double-flowered marguerite. *Chrysanthemum maximum* 'Esther Read' was raised by her father, Horace Postal Read after fifteen years of painstaking, rigid selection. It has been much used as a cut flower, unfortunately in many cases dyed to give bright, unnatural-coloured flowers!

The *Delphinium* 'Rev E Lascelles' perpetuates the memory of the Rev Edwin Lascelles, who was Rector of Holy Trinity Church at Newton St Loe, in Somerset from 1878 to 1904, and later at Midhurst, Sussex where he died in 1923.

He was a keen amateur grower of zonal pelargoniums, begonias and delphiniums, and the delphinium which bears his name occurred as a chance plant in a box of seedlings. Perhaps the rector was particularly fortunate in having as his gardener no less a person than Mr C F Langdon, who in 1900 went into business

Potentilla 'Katherine Dykes'

Mrs Katherine Dykes, after whom the well-known *potentilla* is named.

with Mr J B Blackmore. All growers of begonias and delphiniums know of the success of that partnership at the Tiverton Hill Nursery at Bath, where we can still see some fine displays of delphiniums and large-flowered tuberous begonias. Over the years these nurseries have developed many of our best varieties of both these types of plant.

Bearded iris are always a spectacular sight in June, but the colour range and size of bloom has not always been as we have it today. About 1920 William Rikatson Dykes, secretary of the Royal Horticultural Society, raised a yellow one, and from this went on to raise a golden-yellow one. His final success flowered for the first time a few months after his death in 1925 — it became known as 'W R Dykes', and was a forerunner of many of the yellows which we know today.

Sometime earlier, Mr Dykes had noticed a seedling potentilla, growing between two others in their garden; it was assumed that the parentage was *Potentilla fruticosa x P friedrichensi*. Later, following the death of Mrs Dykes, Gwendolyn Anley, the well-known gardening writer, was asked to select a plant from the Dykes garden, and she chose this potentilla.

She exhibited it at the Royal Horticultural Society where it received an Award of Merit, subsequently also receiving an Award of Garden Merit. Today it is still one of the most popular shrubby potentillas, and of course still bears the name P 'Katherine Dykes'. It has large, soft, warm-yellow flowers which are carried over a long flowering season.

A gem for the rock garden is *Campanula garganica* 'W H Paine', which received an award of merit in 1914. Mr Paine was the manager at Tully Nursery, Kildare, in Ireland. The plant was introduced about 1910, having been originally supplied as a *Campanula garganica* seedling from the famous Backhouse nursery in York some years earlier.

It was on a spring day in 1993 that we drove up the gravel drive of a Leicester-shire garden. On getting out of the car I rang the door bell and was introduced to a lady I had known for almost half a century, but had never met.

Potentilla 'Katherine Dykes'.

12

Eileen May Robinson with her father, who raised 'her' pyrethrum, with his MBE for services to horticulture; and (below) the *pyrethrum* 'Eileen May Robinson'.

In the early 1920s Herbert Robinson, who had the Victoria Nursery at Burbage in Leicestershire, was selecting forms of the herbaceous pyrethrums, a plant which botanists tell us we should now call *Tanacetum coccineum*. One of his best, a large single-flowered pink, became a well-known cut-flower plant, and has continued to be popular in many gardens to the present time. He named it after his daughter 'Eileen May Robinson', who was a baby at the time. Herbert Robinson was awarded the MBE for his services to horticulture, and the National Rose Society gave him the Queen Mary Gold Medal for his work with roses.

I have known the pyrethrum for almost all my life: now I was standing in front of the lady, and talking with her about her father and her life, one enriched by her love of gardening and painting.

13

Opposite Page Top: Richard Turner of Slough, whose nursery introduced both Cox's Orange Pippin and also the old-fashioned garden pink 'Mrs Sinkins'.

Opposite Page Bottom: The church at Harmondsworth where Richard Cox is buried.

Below: Cox's Orange Pippin, still one of Britain's best-loved apples.

2.
An Apple a Day

We are fortunate to have such a wide selection of apples readily available in this country, and many of the most popular ones came into being purely by chance — by someone recognising what was to them an attractively flavoured fruit.

Very little is known about the origin of 'Cox's Orange Pippin', but Cox himself really did exist. Richard Cox was born in either 1776 or 1777, and apparently became a brewer at Bermondsey until he retired to Colnbrook about 1820. In the 1841 census he is listed as living at Lawn Cottage, along with his wife, two maid servants, a boy for domestic work and three labourers.

The house, with a pleasant Georgian exterior, was situated on the north side of the Bath road, between the railway station and the village of Colnbrook. The original 'Cox's Orange Pippin' tree grew in the vegetable garden, about fifty yards from the house, in full view of the central ground floor windows. This tree blew down in 1911, and the house itself has since been demolished and the whole site redeveloped.

The *Garden* magazine of the 27th May 1876 gives the following account of how the tree came into being: 'Mr Turner, of the Royal Nurseries, Slough, informs us that this apple was raised by Mr Cox of Lawn Cottage, Colnbrook in 1830. Of two pips of "Ribston" sown in a pot by Mr Cox, one turned out to be "Cox's Orange Pippin", and the other "Cox's Pomona" — both remarkably fine apples.'

'Cox's Orange Pippin' was originally put into commerce by Messrs Small but the sales at that time were only local. The variety was later taken up by Mr Charles Turner of Slough, a nurseryman who introduced many fine plants.

The first mention of the variety in horticultural literature appears to have been in the *Gardeners' Chronicle* of the 31st October 1857, in a report on the Horticultural Society's Grand Fruit Exhibition, held at Willis's Rooms on Saturday the 24th October:

'Cox's Orange Pippin'

'In the class of single dishes of dessert kinds (of apples) the first prize was awarded to Mr Simpson, gardener to Lady Molyneux, Stoke Farm, Slough, for Cox's Orange Pippin, a medium sized, warm-looking, brownish-red variety with a yellow crisp flesh of most exquisite flavour. This was found on this occasion to be greatly superior to the "Ribston", with fine specimens of which it was carefully compared.'

The judges' decision in passing over the 'Ribston Pippin' in favour of a variety previously unknown was criticised, but after that the 'Cox's Orange Pippin' rapidly became popular.

Ann Cox died on the 9th February 1837, in her seventy-sixth year, and is buried in the churchyard at Harmondsworth, about two miles from Colnbrook. Richard Cox died on the 20th May 1845, in his seventy-ninth year, and is buried in the same grave, near to the north-east corner of the church — a table-top memorial clearly marks the grave.

In 1900 the *Gardeners' Chronicle* had a contribution from Charles Dennis relating to a conversation said to have taken place twenty-five years earlier with Charles Turner. It claims Mr Turner took from one of his large pockets some fruits of Cox's Orange Pippin, and handed one to Mr Dennis to taste, saying to him: 'The best friend I ever had, for it has put me £4000 into my pocket. I never go to bed without one under my pillow, when I can get one.' Mr Dennis then asked Mr Turner to tell him its history, which he did as follows: 'Some years ago a neighbour of mine, Mr Cox, a builder in a small way of business at Langley, was spending Christmas Day with his wife, and in the course of the day an apple was eaten by his wife which so pleased her that she determined to sow the pip, which she did in a flower pot. In course of time two seeds germinated and the seedlings were planted in the garden, one of which died before bearing fruit, and the other was the present tree from which the graft was taken that bore the fruit you are now eating. I watched the tree grow, and tested the quality of its fruit with regard to flavour and keeping, and found it so good that I determined to acquire the entire stock, which I did at a cost of £40.'

Across the world in Australia, another apple made its debut in a similar way. Maria Ann Sherwood and her husband-to-be, Thomas Smith, were both born in Sussex, Maria at Peasmarsh in 1800, and Thomas at Bickley. Together they grew hops. The marriage produced six children — four sons and two daughters — and to find a new life they travelled aboard the *Lady Nugent* in 1838 to Australia. They set up home in the Ryde District of New South Wales, not far from the now-important city of Sydney. Mrs Smith's daughters both married local apple-growers — Sarah to Henry Johnston, and Maria Ann to James Spurway. These two men, half-brothers, were later to take a leading part in the development of the apple, after the death of their mother-in-law.

By the 1860s Mrs Smith had long been a popular figure in the Ryde-Eastwood

'Granny Smith'

Above: Granny Smith, born in Sussex and who is buried in St Anne's Churchyard at Ryde in Australia.

Right: today her memory is kept alive in her adopted town by Granny Smith Park and by the Granny Smith Festival.

Opposite Page: the original Bramley apple tree, still growing in a garden in Southwell.

16

district, and as an older woman was affectionately known as 'Granny'. Since her husband had become a semi-invalid, 'Granny' took on the task of taking the produce from her farm into the city markets.

The way in which she acquired the seeds of her apple is a matter of controversy, but it is believed that she was given some fruits of a French crab variety, which had originated in Tasmania. She must have been pleased with the cooking qualities of the apples because she later planted the pips. One tree grew as a result, eventually producing blossom and fruit — she believed she had a good apple, a good cooker!

Her sons-in-law and another fruit grower, Edward Gallard, began the first significant cultivation of the apple and for some years it was regarded purely as a culinary apple, since in the coastal areas where it was grown it seldom had the opportunity to reach full maturity. In 1895 large plantings were made in the Bathurst district, where the weather was colder and drier, and here the apple's potential as a dessert apple was at last realised — it reaches full maturity when the skin turns yellow and then the apple's flavour is at its peak. The *Agricultural Gazette* at this time referred to the apple as 'Granny Smith's Seedling' — the Granny Smith's apple had arrived!

Part of her property in Eastwood has now been turned into a park — Granny Smith Park — as a memorial to its former owner, but her greatest memorial is her apple.

In Australia they really have no other culinary apple but 'Granny Smith', but of course in the British Isles we have the 'Bramley'!

In about 1856 Henry Merryweather, son of the founder of H Merryweather & Sons, was about seventeen years old and was working in his father's newly-established nursery. One day he saw George Musson, gardener to the Rev Alfred Tatham, vicar choral or minor canon of Southwell Minster, carrying a basket of particularly good-looking apples. They had come from Rev Tatham's orchard, which was near to the nursery.

When Henry Merryweather was ninety years old, a presentation was made to him, and in his response he told this story which was related in the press: 'I said, "What have you got there?", He [George Musson] said, "Bramley's apple". I said "Where does it grow?", and he said, "In Mr

RYDE MUNICIPAL COUNCIL

CARNIVALE '86

GRANNY SMITH FESTIVAL COMMITTEE

Carnivale is a state-wide multi-cultural festival celebrated at a local level every Spring.

This year Ryde Council is combining Carnivale with a new local "Granny Smith Festival". A gala festival day centred on Ryde Park will take place in late September as part of these celebrations.

A community festival committee will be responsible for planning, organising and running the festival.

A public meeting will be held at 6.30 pm on Monday, May 12, 1986 at the Ryde Centenary Library, Devlin Street, Ryde, to discuss ideas for this year's festivities and to elect a festival committee. People from a migrant background are particularly encouraged to attend

We need your p...

Bramley's seedling

Bramley's garden, back of his house". I went to look at the tree in full fruit. I had not seen the like of it before. I asked for grafts and he said fetch what you want. I then made enquiries about this apple but could not get to hear that the wonder had got away anywhere. I set to work to work up a stock . . . '

On that day in 1856 Musson was actually coming from Tatham's orchard, and although the original tree was growing in Mr Bramley's garden, the apples in the basket had been gathered from a tree in Rev Tatham's orchard, which subsequently became the property of Messrs Merryweather.

When the Royal Horticultural Society's fruit committee met on the 6th December 1876, they had before them from 'Messrs Merryweather & Son of Southwell a new kitchen apple called Bramley's Seedling, of large size and excellent quality. It was highly commended'.

But who was Mr Bramley? Matthew Bramley was born in 1795 or 1796, the son of a cordwainer (shoemaker). In 1844 he was the keeper of the White Lion Inn, Easthorpe, Southwell, and later he became a butcher. The title deeds show that he purchased what is now known as Bramley Tree Cottage (73 Church Street) on the 28th November 1846, and lived there until his death in 1871. He is buried at Southwell Minster. As he had only lived in the house for ten years before the apples were noticed by Henry Merryweather, it is very doubtful that Bramley did in fact raise the apple which bears his name.

In the report of the Royal Horticultural Society's apple and pear conference for 1888, Mr Merryweather gave Bramley the credit for having raised the apple, but in his own catalogue of 1892 he went into the matter more fully, stating that the variety was 'a chance seedling from pips, sown in a flower pot, by a lady named Brailsford. She planted it out but did not see the fruit. After her death some 40 or 50 years ago the house and garden passes into the possession of a person named Bramley, and this tree fruited in his time'.

There is a local tradition that the original tree came from a pip sown by Elizabeth Brailsford, who lived at the cottage before Bramley. The title deeds show that in 1809 the cottage was the property of Charles Brailsford and that upon his death in 1812 it became the property of his wife, Elizabeth. She died in 1837, leaving the property to her daughters, Mary Ann Hindley and Diana Aram. They sold it in 1838, and it was subsequently purchased by Matthew Bramley in 1846. It therefore seems certain that the lady who sowed the pip was Mrs Charles Brailsford, although there is a suggestion that it might have been sown by her daughter, Mary Ann, while she was living at home, possibly between 1809 and 1813.

In the 1970s it was rumoured that the EEC would stop the marketing of the 'Bramley', but a vigorous campaign was mounted to help the 'Bramley' into Europe, and one of the leaders of this was Mrs Celia Steven, Henry Merryweather's great-granddaughter. Today at the nursery there is a small but very

interesting museum which shows the story of the apple and the nursery.

On many occasions horticulture has had good reason to thank the clergy for their interest in the world of nature, and plant life in particular. The apple 'Ellison's Orange' was the child of a vicarage garden.

Charles Christopher Ellison was born on the 26th November 1834, the youngest son of Colonel Richard and Elizabeth Ellison of Boultham Hall, near Lincoln. After an education at Rugby School and Trinity College, Cambridge, he was appointed vicar of Bracebridge in 1863. Soon afterwards he also became a guardian of the poor for the parish which is now a suburb of Lincoln. In 1870 he was elected chairman of the Lincoln Board of Guardians, which comprised representatives of nearly one hundred city and country parishes, a position he held for nearly thirty years.

Rev C C Ellison was a man of many attributes. His great hobby was turning ivory and the delicate beauty of the miniatures he produced was quite outstanding. His best lathe was one he designed himself and which took nearly three and a half years to construct. So accurate was its performance it would work to a thousandth of an inch, and so enthusiastic was he about his hobby that he not only worked his pieces but also recorded, in two volumes, all the details of their design. In addition to his work with the board of guardians, he was a magistrate for many years. In the world of sport he also excelled, being a fine cricketer and archer, and he was at home with both gun and salmon rod. Richard Ellison, the Kent and England cricketer, is his great-grandson.

His garden was often open to local enthusiasts and it is said to have contained

Ellison's own handwriting describes
his apple.

19

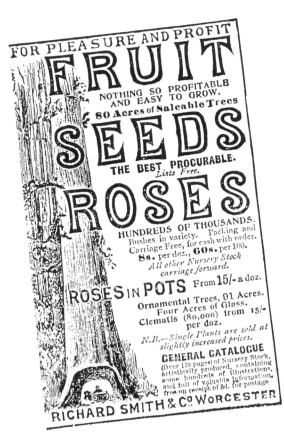

Richard Smith & Co of Worcester were well-known nurserymen in the nineteenth century and introduced the 'Worcester Pearmain' apple.

'Ellison's Orange'

several thousand roses, but his pride in this sphere was the introduction of the eating apple which bears his name. Once again his patience was rewarded, for its introduction followed sixteen years of experimentation. Apparently Mr Ellison discussed with Mr Wipf, gardener to his brother-in-law, Mr Shuttleworth, at Hartsholme Hall, the idea of developing a new apple and the two decided to cross 'Cox's Orange Pippin' with a very old French variety called 'Calville Blanche' — the result was a dessert apple which cropped regularly and heavily. Such was its quality that it won an Award of Merit when placed before the Royal Horticultural Fruit Committee in 1911.

The original cross first fruited in the garden of the old Bracebridge Vicarage, renamed the Manse when Mr Ellison retired in 1900. In 1908 Mr Ellison wrote to some of the leading nurserymen inviting offers for 'about 600 good grafts — probably 1000 — could be found', he said. 'I desire to sell it for the benefit of the gardener (not my own) who helped me to raise it.' Most of the firms declined to bid, but the stock was purchased, and the variety distributed, by Messrs Pennell & Sons. The original tree was eventually uprooted to make way for a housing estate!

The Rev Charles Ellison died in 1912. A writer in *The Times* summed him up in these words: 'It was as a man he was remarkable. Great in stature, great in heart, the keynote of his character was his downright straightforwardness.' The obituary in the *Field* magazine read: 'He belongs to the select company of great-hearted parsons such as Charles Kingsley, who in life were like a wholesome moorland breeze, and who in death will be honoured as long as Englishmen fear God, honour the King, and love the open air.'

Today, unfortunately, we remember only his apple!

A note in the *Gardeners' Chronicle* on the 3rd January 1874, under an item headed 'The new fruits of 1873', states: 'In the Worcester Pearmain, raised from the Red Quarrenden, we have a very beautiful highly-coloured early dessert fruit, which cannot fail to come into general cultivation.'

How right they were! But how did it come about? In 1872 Mr Hales had two seedling apples in his fruit and market garden at Swanpool, near Worcester — one had yellow fruit, the other was brightly coloured.

Richard Smith, a nurseryman in Worcester, saw the trees and offered the owner £10 for the exclusive right to remove grafts from the coloured one. In 1873 he took grafting material and worked them onto a number of rootstocks in his nursery, and from these he budded large numbers onto seedling and paradise rootstocks. They were subsequently offered for sale in the *Gardeners' Chronicle* in 1875 at 10s 6d each for maiden trees, and 21s each for pyramid or trained trees.

It was awarded a first class certificate by the Royal Horticultural Society on the 6th October 1875. A coloured plate of it occurs in the *Florist and Pomologist* of June 1876.

The 'Ribston Pippin' was the most widely grown apple in the 1800s. It came from the garden of Ribston Hall, near Wetherby, in Yorkshire. It is included in catalogue lists as far back as 1775.

Legend has it that some pips were brought back from Rouen, in Normandy, about 1690. These were sown at Ribston and five seedlings resulted — two turned out to be crabs and three to be apples. All were planted out at Ribston and grew to the stage where they fruited. The original 'Ribston Pippin' tree blew down in 1810, fracturing the stem about seven feet from the ground, but from the remaining stem new shoots grew and produced fruit. At this time the estate belonged to Sir Henry Goodricke, Bart, who was unfortunately an unreliable source of information. However, in the *Gardeners' Chronicle* of the 14th December 1844 a correspondent suggests that the account is the same as that transmitted to him by Lady Goodriche. This original tree is thought to have finally died about 1932 The 'Ribston Pippin' is said to have been the parent of the 'Cox's Orange Pippin'.

Charles Ross, like a number of head gardeners, followed in his father's footsteps. Charles was born on the Dalmeny Estate in Midlothian, Scotland, in 1824. By 1856 he had also become a head gardener at Fairlawn, Tonbridge in Kent, and to celebrate the end of the Crimean War, in that year, he planted a *Sequoia gigantea*. In 1860 he moved to Welford Park, near Newbury, where he stayed until he retired in 1908, at the age of eighty-four!

The variety which bears his name was introduced in 1899, the same year that it received an award of merit from the Royal Horticultural Society. Originally it was called 'Thomas Andrew Knight', after the second president of the Royal Horticultural Society from 1810 to 1838, but later it reverted to the name of its raiser, Charles Ross. It is described as a cross between 'Cox's Orange Pippin' and 'Peasgood Nonsuch'.

BEST LATE APPLE.

WE CAN STRONGLY RECOMMEND OUR NEW APPLE
"NEWTON WONDER,"
as the best late Apple in cultivation; fruit keeps till June;
large, well-coloured, perfect form, splendid cooking quality;
tree a vigorous grower, free from canker, and very productive.
Awarded First-class Certificate, R.H.S., Dec. 1887.
Now Widely Known. Descriptive Catalogue of Fruits
on Application.
J. R. PEARSON & SONS, Chilwell Nurseries, Notts.

An early advert for the 'Newton Wonder' apple by the nursery who introduced it to apple lovers.

The Hardinge Arms where the 'Newton Wonder' apple first appeared as a seedling on its thatched roof.

'Newton Wonder'

Charles Ross was awarded the Victoria Medal of Honour by the Royal Horticultural Society and died in 1917 at the age of ninety-two.

Many new varieties of apple have resulted from the discovery of an outstanding fruit, often by an amateur, rather than as the result of a long breeding programme. One important new variety of the 1960s, 'Discovery', really did come in that way! Denis Todhunter recalls how, along with an Essex fruit-grower, Robin Leslie, he called to see a Mrs Dummer at Langham, near Colchester in August 1960. The tree growing in her garden was then about ten to fifteen years old and was carrying a good crop of well-coloured fruit. They were impressed not only by the quality of the apples but also by its freedom from pest and disease, especially as no chemical sprays had been used.

Mr Dummer had died some years earlier. He had been a local fruit-farm worker who enjoyed raising seedlings in his spare time, and he must have thought this one was particularly promising for he planted it in his own garden. Its parentage is unknown but is thought to be a cross between 'Beauty of Bath' and 'Worcester Pearmain'.

At first the apple, introduced by Matthews Fruit Trees Ltd of Thurston, near Bury St. Edmunds, was known as 'Dummer's Seedling', then as 'Thurston August'; before being introduced as 'Discovery'. It has had a remarkable rise to commercial popularity, becoming the main English early eating apple.

Derbyshire is not generally regarded as a great fruit-growing county but it has at least one claim to fame. The 'Newton Wonder' apple originated at King's Newton near Melbourne.

William Taylor is said to have raised it in 1868, according to an item in the *Gardeners' Chronicle* of the 21st December 1895. Legend has it that it first appeared as a seedling on the thatched roof of an old inn, the Hardinge Arms, and was taken down and for some time grown in a plant pot in the back yard, afterwards being transferred to the garden. It is said that it came into bearing about 1876. Taylor budded and grafted trees of the variety and then sold fifty to Messrs Pearson of Chilwell who introduced it to commerce. So that it might be exhibited before the Royal Horticultural Society on the 13th December 1887, Taylor provided them with a dish of fruits.

It is a distinctive variety both in its growth and in its fruit. The leaves are easily recognised, being large and broad with a peculiar sage-like appearance. In every sense it is a late apple, blooming late, not really ready for picking until October and under suitable conditions keeping well; indeed if kept until February or March it becomes a good dessert apple.

Little is known about the 'Blenheim Orange' except that it was grown from a pip by a Mr Kempster of Woodstock, near to Blenheim Estate. It first came to notice in 1818.

James Grieve went to work for Dicksons Nursery in Edinburgh in 1859 and stayed with them until 1896, when he started his own business with his two sons.

Whilst at Dicksons he was involved with hybridisation (as well as rising to the position of nursery manager), particularly with achimenes, carnations, phlox, rhododendron and also fruits, the apple 'James Grieve' being named after him in 1890. Edward A Bunyard, in his book *A Handbook of Fruits*, described 'James Grieve' as 'a most excellent fruit, quite the best of its season'.

One could say that the judgement of Bunyard on such an apple was indeed an accreditation of its quality for he was long associated with the firm of George Bunyard & Co. of Maidstone, which was founded in 1796. It was in 1869 that they purchased the Allington Nurseries, which are immortalised in the apple 'Allington Pippin'.

Our final apple is one raised by Messrs Laxton of Bedford, and was awarded the RHS Cup for the best seedling apple of 1921 and 1922. Its name is 'Lord Lambourne' and commemorates its namesake, who was president of the Royal Horticultural Society from 1917 until his death in 1928.

The longevity of most of this band of 'apple pioneers' would indeed seem to prove the old adage 'an apple a day keeps the doctor away'!

Above Top: James Harvey Logan.

Above: On the American continent the Williams pear is known as the Bartlett pear and is here featured on a Canadian stamp.

Opposite Page Top: Conference pear.

Opposite Page Middle: 'Williams' pear.

Opposite Page Bottom: An advert for the new 'Conference' pear.

3.
A Fruit Cocktail

James Harvey Logan was the seventh of the eight children born to Samuel McCampbell and Mary Elizabeth Logan at Rockville, Indiana. Although both parents were born in Kentucky, they were of Scottish ancestry. James was born on the 8th December 1841.

On growing up he taught for a year, then took a job as driver of an ox team for the Overland Telegraph Company. Some time later he moved to California and in December 1863 started reading Law at San José. In 1865 he was admitted to the Bar, and three years later he moved to Santa Cruz where almost immediately he became deputy district attorney. For the next twelve years he was a judge of the Superior Court in Santa Cruz County.

It was not until 1880 that he started an experimental fruit and vegetable garden at his home in Santa Cruz. That year he planted every variety of blackberry and raspberry he could obtain. Among these were the Texas Early blackberry (*Rubus villosus*) and the Californian dewberry (*R ursinus*, a sub-variety of *R canadensis*, a two-sexed variety). These were planted side by side to secure a hybrid. Next to these was a Red Antwerp raspberry (*Rubus idaeus*).

In 1881 the plants bore fruit and the seed of the *Rubus ursinus* was taken and sown. About 300 seedlings grew and in the spring of 1883 he noticed one seedling unlike the others, indeed it had a striking resemblance to the raspberry. In May of that year the fruit began to ripen. It had a flavour and character all of its own. Logan also noticed that the flowers were perfectly formed and self-pollinating, and although the seeds germinated the resultant plants were generally of poor quality. (Therefore the plant is best propagated by tip layering.)

In an article in the *Gardeners' Chronicle*, written in the early part of this century, it was suggested that the best way to treat the fruit of the loganberry is to place them, when mature, in sugar for twenty-four hours, and then eat them. James Logan eventually gave plant material of the loganberry to Professor Wickson of the University of California for free distribution and today it is grown in many parts of the world.

The Royal Horticultural Society recommended that the 'Logan Berry' be given an Award of Merit. Judge Logan died at his home in Oakland, California, in 1928.

The best-known grape grown in amateurs' greenhouses must be the Black Hamburgh. We know little of its origin, except that it was imported to this country by John Warner, in the early part of the eighteenth century. Apparently this is the same John Warner, mentioned in the *History and Survey of London*, who lived in East Lane, Rotherhithe, and who died on the 24th February 1760. He was a London merchant and had his vineyard at Rotherhithe.

The number of pears commonly known to gardeners today is fairly limited when compared with fifty or a hundred years ago. In those earlier days 'Beurre Hardy' was well known, and is widely referred to in old gardening books. It was raised by Monsieur Bonnet of Boulogne, and named in honour of Monsieur Hardy, who was the director of the Luxembourg Gardens. It was first exhibited at a meeting of the British Pomological Society in 1858. At that time it was a little-known variety but took second prize, and earned the comment 'considered of being more generally cultivated' — it certainly was for many years to come.

In 1885 at a National Pear Conference, held at Chiswick, T S Rivers & Son of Sawbridgeworth introduced a new variety. It was the only newcomer to receive a certificate from the Royal Horticultural Society, and so they decided to simply call it 'Conference'. This lovely fruit, with its dark russet skin and rich salmon-coloured flesh which melts in the mouth when ripe and juicy, is deservedly well-known. However, the Williams' pear is much older, being raised almost certainly before 1770 by a Mr Wheeler, a schoolmaster of Aldermaston in Berkshire. Wheeler sold it to a Mr Williams, a nurseryman of Turnham Green, in Middlesex. In 1799 it was introduced to America by Enoch Bartlett of Dorchester, near Boston, and became known as the 'Bartlett' pear.

When you buy a can of tinned pears they are, of course, always labelled as 'Bartlett' pears, never as Williams!

Two well-established varieties of blackcurrant are those known as 'Boskoop Giant' and 'Wellington XXX.' The former was originated by Mr Hoogendyk of

NEW SEEDLING PEAR, "CONFERENC RIVERS.

Certificated by the Royal Horticultural Society.

Fruit large, pyriform; skin dark green and russet; flesh salmon coloured, melting, juicy, and rich. Tree robust and hardy, making a strong healthy growth on the Pear and Quince stocks. Very prolific, a good garden and orchard fruit, and a valuable market sort. It ripens from the first to the third week in November. Strong trees, 3s. 6d. each.

The **DESCRIPTIVE CATALOGUE** of **FRUITS**, post-free, 3d. | The **DESCRIPTIVE CATALOGUE** of **ROSES**, gratis.

THOMAS RIVERS & SON, THE NURSERIES, SAWBRIDGEWORTH, HERTS.

Telegrams—" RIVERS & SON, Sawbridgeworth." *Station for Nurseries*—HARLOW, G.E.R.

Gooseberry 'Whinham's Industry'

PRICE LIST

FOR

PRIVATE FAMILIES.

6, 9, 12 & 18-gallon casks supplied at

the undermentioned Prices.

		Per Gallon.
		s.	d.
X ALE	@	1	0
XX BEER	@	1	2
XXX Do.	@	1	4
XXXX Do.	@	1	6
BITTER BEER	@	1	7
FITZWILLIAM	@	1	7
WHARNCLIFFE ALE	@	1	10
PORTER	@	1	2
INVALID STOUT	@	1	4

LIGHT BITTER BEER @ 1/2 per gallon
specially recommended for Family use.

Tennant Brothers, whose beer inspired the name for a black-currant when it was linked with that of Captain Wellington, who is pictured below.

Boskoop in Holland. It was introduced to the British gardening public in 1895 by Messrs Bunyard of Maidstone.

The blackcurrant 'Wellington XXX' has an interesting story and celebrates a man who made a notable contribution to fruit growing. Robert Wellington was born in 1890, and in 1913 he helped to found the embryo Wye College Fruit Experiment Station. Some of the early work involved the collection and development of Paradise rootstocks with a view to assessing their value as root systems for commercial apple varieties.

After being invalided out of the East Kent Yeomanry, with the rank of captain, following the battle of the Somme, Wellington was posted to work at the Ministry of Food Production. It was then, as director of the station, that he worked on strawberries, blackcurrants, plums and cooking apples. In those early days of the station he is said to have sown some seeds of blackcurrants in kipper boxes. One of the resultant seedlings was 'Wellington XXX' — it so happened that Wellington and some of his colleagues were drinking XXX beer when they were trying to think of a name!

A further connection is the blackcurrant 'Amos Late Black' — Jesse Amos was Wellington's 'foreman recorder'. He was involved with the work of East Malling Research Station for over thirty years, and the Amos Memorial Lecture was inaugurated in memory of him and his work.

Malling is a well known prefix to varieties of raspberry and apple rootstocks. 'Malling Jewel' was the first of a long list of raspberry varieties introduced by Norman Grubb. The Malling rootstocks were standard for many years, their vigour being distinguished by the allocation of a Roman numeral, two of the most commonly used being Malling II and IX. These have been followed by the Malling Merton types, distinguished by the prefix MM, the most common ones being MM109 and MM104. The original Malling rootstocks enabled one to choose, for the first time, a rootstock with a known vigour, the Malling Merton ones gave the added value of disease resistance.

One of the most famous gooseberries at the turn of the present century was 'Whinham's Industry', which was raised by Robert Whinham of Morpeth. He was born in the early years of the nineteenth century and died in 1858. As a tenant of the Earl of Carlisle, he occupied Allery Banks Gardens at Morpeth. He is buried in Morpeth churchyard. The circumstances as to how the variety came about are unclear, but in the *Gardeners' Chronicle* of 1893 it was reported that it was being exported to the United States and Canada, France, Germany and Holland — the Dutch then sent back large quantities of berries to the Newcastle fruit market! Mr Richard Smith of Worcester, who introduced the apple 'Worcester Pearmain', also introduced this plant to the continent of America.

At that period, it was the sale of the young fruit bushes, rather than the goose-berries, which was the main financial benefit in the North-East of England and in

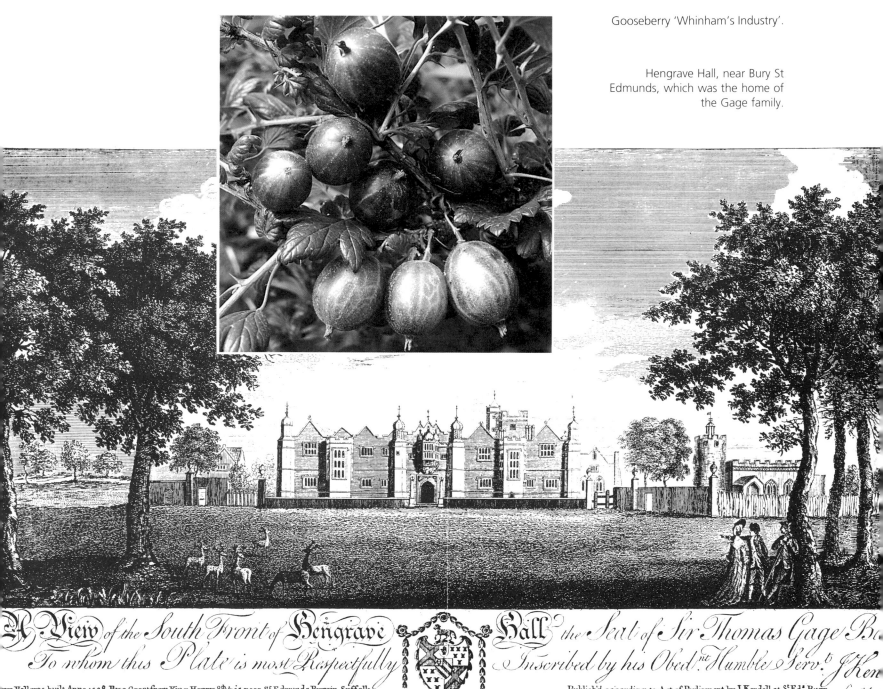

Gooseberry 'Whinham's Industry'.

Hengrave Hall, near Bury St Edmunds, which was the home of the Gage family.

A View of the South Front of Hengrave Hall the Seat of Sir Thomas Gage B[.]
To whom this Plate is most Respectfully Inscribed by his Obed.nt Humble Serv.t J.Ken[.]

[Hengra]ve Hall was built Anno 1538. By a Grant from King Henry 8th & is near St. Edmunds Bury in Suffolk.   Publish'd according to Act of Parliament by J. Kendall at St. Ed.s Bury.

27

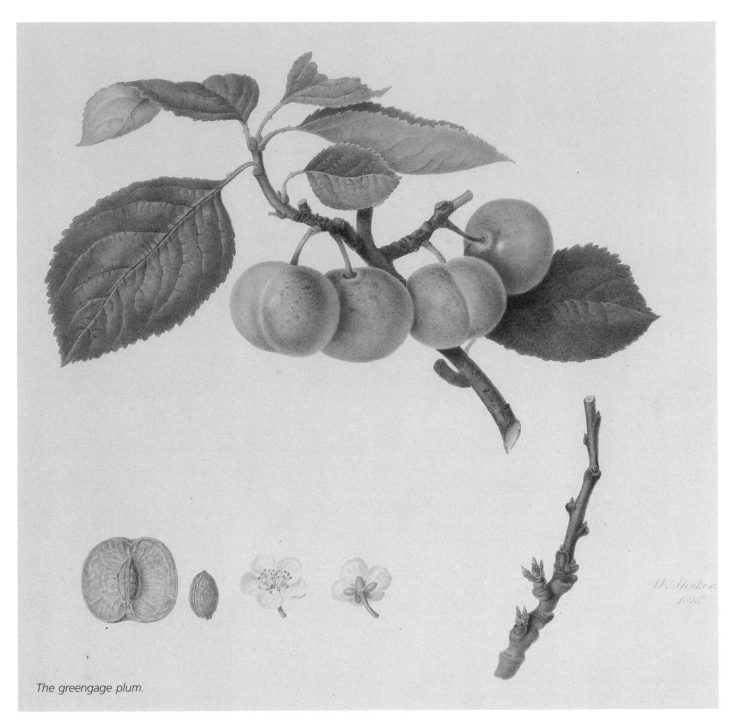

The greengage plum.

a report in 1891 Messrs W Fell & Co of Hexham had 400,000 one, two and three year old bushes available. Initially bushes were always produced by layering but subsequently they were produced by cuttings.

'Whinham's Industry' was particularly heavy in bearing, an old bush cropping up to four stones; a Hexham fruit grower, at that time, had picked twenty-six tons of fruit from a 3 acre plantation! The fruit are of a dark dusky red colour when ripe.

And so it seems that many of the fruits we enjoy today have been enjoyed by generations before us.

Probably the earliest of these is the plum 'Green Gage'. Where or when it originated we do not know, but it was certainly cultivated in France during the reign of King Francois I (1494–1547) and there it was named in honour of his queen, 'Reine Claude'. It is still so called on the Continent and in America, but in Britain it acquired the name 'Green Gage'. Why?

In the eighteenth century Peter Collinson, who was a well-known Quaker and horticulturist, wrote a memorandum, later published in *Hortus Collinsonianus* in 1843: 'I was on a visit to Sir William Gage, at Hengrave, near Bury (St Edmunds); he was then near 70; he told me that he first brought over, from France, the Grosse Reine Claude, and introduced it into England, and in compliment to him the plum was called the Green Gage; this was about the year 1725. P. Collinson'

According to the *History and Antiquities of Hengrave*, Sir William Gage, second baronet, died on the 8th February 1727 in his seventy-first year. This would seem to confirm that it was about 1725 when Peter Collinson was at Hengrave and had the origin of the name explained to him.

In Philip Miller's *Gardeners and Florists Dictionary*, which was published in 1724, 'Green Gage' appears in an appendix to volume II in a list of 'Several Curious Sorts of Plumbs'. The same list contains 'Reine Claude', but neither appear in the body of the book, although there is reference to a plum 'Queen Claudia'. This proves that the plum was in existence and well-known prior to 1724.

There is a tradition among the Jesuits that a Father Gage sent the original tree to Hengrave, but it is not known who he was — he may have been a relative of Sir William Gage, whose body lies at Hengrave. Although the plum is associated with Sir William it is suggested that he was neither the first nor the only person to have imported it.

Today Hengrave Hall is, to all outward appearances, as it would have been in those distant days, but it is now used as a Christian Study Centre.

Unfortunately, some fruits have a 'lost past'. Among them is the 'Victoria' plum which was discovered in a garden in Alderton, in Sussex, and the 'Doyenne du Comice' pear which was raised in the garden of the Comice Horticole at Angers, the original tree first fruiting in 1849.

THE

Gardeners' Chronicle.

SATURDAY, SEPTEMBER 17, 1892.

BODNANT.

BODNANT is situated on the east side of the Conway Valley, within the influence of the sea breeze, but protected in the lower parts by the high hills. From the lawn a fine prospect, embracing about 60 miles of mountain scenery, is to be seen. The soil is not rich, being shallow, and resting upon the Wenlock flags and shales of the upper silurian formation. The garden was originally designed and laid out by the late Mr. Milner, but in recent years the taste of the proprietor, H. D. Pochin, Esq., aided by the skill of his gardener, Mr. Saunderson, has been mainly directed to the beautifying of the glen. The higher parts are planted with hardwooded deciduous trees, which afford sufficient shelter to the specimen Conifers, the latter making very rapid growth, and are of a beautiful colour. The effect of the Coniferæ is much improved by the judicious mixture of bright deciduous trees and shrubs, such as the rich purple Prunus Pissardii and purple Hazel, clumps of Cornus sanguinea, scarlet Dogwood, and groups of flowering shrubs, such as Berberis, Rubus, Cotoneaster, Hypericum, &c., giving brightness without suggesting any artificial character to the place. Considerable labour has been spent in ... the banks of the trout stream ... for what is now a ...

4.
Plants of Famous Gardens

As a nation we have a great heritage of beautiful gardens which have developed over many years. Conceived and nurtured by their owners and their gardeners, they have gradually evolved to the present day. Many of them are visited by thousands of visitors each year who delight in the beauty of the overall design, the majesty of the mature trees, and the colourful mix of the various flowers in their season. Several of these gardens have outstanding plants that have developed either naturally or from seeds sent to the owner by those collecting plant material and seeds in distant lands.

One such garden is Bodnant in North Wales. A combination of the mature, majestic trees and mighty mountains make a lovely backcloth for a truly beautiful garden. At Bodnant there are wonderful views across the Snowdon range of mountains, stretching for up to sixty miles, and many of the trees date back to the last years of the eighteenth century.

In 1875 Henry Pochin, great-grandfather of the present Lord Aberconway, bought the house and estate. It was he who planted most of the large conifers, and with the help of Mr Milner, a well known landscape architect of the day, created many of the features which are now mature.

Mr Pochin's daughter, the first Lady Aberconway, increased the range of flowering plants but, perhaps more importantly, introduced her son to the garden, giving him the opportunity to spend his life supervising its development.

Even in those early days it was well-known, both for its natural beauty and for its neatness and created landscapes. In 1892 the *Gardeners' Chronicle* featured the garden in an article listing many of its plants, not just the trees and shrubs, but also its apples and the tender subjects in its glasshouses. There were bunches of grapes eighteen inches long and 'well shouldered', standard apples planted by outbuildings which had their branches trained up on to the roofs! From these roof trees, fruits of the variety 'Peasgood's Nonsuch' had weighed in at twenty ounces each.

About 1903, Henry, son of the first Lady Aberconway, was entrusted with the care of the garden. From then onwards their exhibits of rare and choice plants were frequently seen at the Royal Horticultural Society's shows at Vincent Square in London. Henry gave over fifty years to the task, becoming a gardener of immense knowledge, and also president of the society. Not only has the garden stayed in one family for over a hundred years, but it has also been tended by a

Viburnum x Bodnantense 'Dawn'

succession of 'Puddles' as head gardeners. Mr F C Puddle VMH came to Bodnant in 1920, and has been followed by his son and grandson thus giving a continuous link for over seventy years!

The house and garden was given to the National Trust in 1949, but is still looked after by the Aberconway family. The third Lord Aberconway was president of the Royal Horticultural Society from 1961 until 1984.

Over the years the Aberconways and the Puddles have faithfully contributed to the development of the garden with skill and love, and today the present members of those families can see the large numbers of visitors, from all walks of life and all parts of the world, enjoying its beauty.

Of the plants associated with the garden, perhaps the best known is *Viburnum X bodnantense* 'Dawn', a gem among the winter flowering shrubs, one which arose in the garden as a result of a cross between *Viburnum farreri* and *V grandiflorum*. Many of the rhododendrons raised in the garden have been named after members of the family. Perhaps the best known is *Rhododendron* 'Elizabeth', named after the third Lord Aberconway's elder sister — this is a particularly fine cultivar which has received the Award of Merit, First-Class Certificate and also the Award of Garden Merit. The plant is of a dwarf nature, producing a spreading shrub which bears clusters of rich, dark-red trumpet-shaped flowers in April.

The wide spectrum of plant interest which has taken place at Bodnant ranges from such diverse groups as hybrid *Cyprepediums* developed by F C Puddle to *Clivia kewensis* 'Bodnant Yellow', as well as the hardy plants which have been previously mentioned.

A much younger garden, and one associated with only one man, is Hidcote in the Cotswolds. Lawrence Waterbury Johnston was born in Paris in 1871, the son of American parents. The Johnstons, who had Scottish connections, came from the north of Ireland. With an early life spent in France, Lawrence must have become accustomed to beauty and culture.

He was educated at home by a tutor, and was always very close to his mother, his father having died while he was still quite young. His mother married again whilst he was in his mid-teens but her second husband died in 1898. He is said to have been dominated by his mother who bought him the property known as Hidcote Bartrim in 1907. Prior to this he had studied at Cambridge University and received a degree in history from Trinity College. In 1900 he became a naturalised British subject and served with the Imperial Yeomanry in South Africa in the Boer War. However, he suffered from weak lungs, and so he moved to Northumberland to become a student farmer.

Undoubtedly his active interest in farming was a factor leading to the purchase of Hidcote. The estate consisted of about 280 acres of farmland, a tiny hamlet of thatched cottages, and a small stone farmhouse.

Opposite Page Top: Bodnant garden, one of the best-loved gardens in North Wales.

Below: *Viburnum bodnantense* 'Dawn', a plant that flowers in the darkest days of winter.

Bottom: Lawrence Johnston, the creator of the famous Hidcote garden.

Clematis 'Hidcote Purple', one of several good plants to have been 'born' within these gardens or associated with them.

His knowledge and interest in gardening had grown rapidly, and fortunately for him, and for us, it was matched by his mother's fortune. By now he was thirty-six years old and gardening had become his chosen hobby. He was also fortunate in having many friends who were passionate and knowledgeable gardeners and who lived close by. Among these were Major Mark Fenwick at Abbotswood, Clarence Elliott who lived near Moreton-in-Marsh, and later the Jack Muirs who came to live at Kiftsgate at the end of the drive leading to Hidcote. This was the birthplace of the extremely vigorous rose, which carries multitudes of small, sweetly-scented, creamy-white flowers, called *Rosa filipes* 'Kiftsgate'.

Little by little the garden grew at Hidcote; it is said that a trainful of lime-free soil came from Surrey for the camellias, rhododendrons and other lime-hating plants! His plantings were entirely original, and acres of rough pasture were turned over and planted up to give botanical and horticultural interest. Johnston involved himself with the work and later went on plant-collecting trips, first to South Africa with Major Collingwood Ingram and then to Yunnan in China with George Forrest, on what was to be Forrest's last journey to that area.

Johnston died in 1958 at Serre de la Madone, but is buried, beside his mother, in Mickleton Churchyard, a mile or two from his beloved Hidcote.

Hidcote Manor was the first garden to be presented to the Committee for the Preservation of Gardens of Outstanding Merit, under the joint auspices of the Royal Horticultural Society and the National Trust. The garden covers ten acres, and although it is a plantsman's garden it also has good aesthetic taste. Two very good plants which have come from the garden are *Rosa* 'Lawrence Johnston', a climbing rose with large semi-double bright yellow flowers, and the better-known *Hypericum* 'Hidcote', a superb garden shrub which produces masses of golden-yellow saucer-shaped flowers from July to October — a plant for *every* garden!

Another garden which has given us one of our much loved-shrubs was Clandon, near Guildford in Surrey. It was the home of Mr A Simmonds, deputy secretary of the Royal Horticultural Society. About 1930 a chance seedling of *Caryopteris mongolica* X *C incana* sprang up and has since become known as *Caryopteris x clandonensis*. In late August and September it carries numerous trusses of violet-blue flowers which are most attractive to bees.

Over the years many gardeners, great gardeners, have not only loved their gardens and their plants but have enthused over them in such a way that others have caught something of their zeal and so the gospel has spread. Perhaps like those early Christians who had to write their experiences down so that others might share their joy, so these great gardeners have made their experience of gardening come alive for others. Some years ago my wife bought me the trilogy of books by E A Bowles — *My Garden in Spring*, *My Garden in Summer*, and *My Garden in Autumn and Winter* — and so I learned more of that great gardener and writer.

Edward Augustus Bowles is said to have gained his first interest in gardening following a visit to the family garden at Myddleton House by Canon Ellacombe. Edward Bowles had just come down from Cambridge University, where he had read theology, to find that, for family reasons, he would be unable to take holy orders.

Around 1890 Bowles started to plan and remake his father's garden. By now he had made friends with such well-known horticultural figures as Reginald Farrer, Rev Wolley-Dod, Sir Thomas Hanbury and many others. As a result he had gained from them some of their experience and knowledge, and no doubt also many plants. He suffered from severe asthma and, as a consequence took annual visits to the high Alps in late spring, always returning with a heavy cargo of plants that he had collected in the wild. However he was not selfish with such riches. Apparently when friends and visitors alike came to his garden, his greeting was 'I hope you have brought a basket with you'. Many of the plants he had collected would be destined for his rock garden, unusual in that it was constructed from Kentish ragstone. The garden at Myddleton House at Enfield thus became a plantsman's garden with a vast range of plants. In the early part of this century, although only ten miles from London, it was set in rural surroundings. The family had settled there in the early nineteenth century; indeed his great grandmother had planted a *Taxodium distichum* on the site not long before 1812, and the house was built a few years later.

E A Bowles, a man not selfish with the riches of his garden, but generous to all.

Below: *Erysimum linifolium* 'Bowles Mauve'.

Bottom: *Philadelphus* 'Beauclerk'.

Pulmonaria 'Bowles Red'

Bowles was a man of many seasons, for he was born in 1865 and lived to be nearly ninety years old. He was a true Victorian in many ways, particularly in his dislike of change, so much so that even in the 1950s he preferred an oil lamp to that of an electric filament. He was also a deeply committed Christian and a great supporter of his church in Enfield.

His garden was particularly rich in kniphofias, geraniums, eremurus, standard wistarias, magnolias, eucalyptus, and those plants of which he had a special knowledge, crocus, colchicum and narcissi. One particular area was called the 'Asylum', because it contained what he called 'demented' plants. These included a twisted hazel, a similarly twisted hawthorn, a fastigiate form of the common elderberry, an oak-leaved variety of the common laburnum, a pigmy ash (*Fraxinus excelsior* 'Atrovirens Nana'), and the one-leaved strawberry (*Fragaria vesca* 'Monophylla') to name but a few!

Today he is remembered for his writings and also for such plants as *Erysimum linifolium* 'Bowles Mauve', *Pulmonaria* 'Bowles Red', *Viola* 'Bowles Black' and *Crocus chrysanthus* 'Snow Bunting', one of a range of crocus cultivars that he selected which were all named after birds — alas many of the others are now unknown in cultivation. *Crocus chrysanthus* 'E A Bowles' was actually raised in the Dutch nurseries of Van Tubergen and named to honour one of England's great gardeners.

The Loders have made a major contribution to gardening in this country, particularly through their involvement with the gardens at Wakehurst Place and Leonardslee.

The name of Wakehurst occurs for the first time in the reign of King Stephen (1135-1154), when Walwerd de Wakehurst rented land from the monks of Battle Abbey in the manor of Apuldram, near Chichester. The first link with Ardingly, where the present garden is located, was then Wakehurst purchased some land in the parish in 1205. There has been a house on the site for over 400 years, although the Loder family did not purchase the property until 1902.

Gerald Loder, who became Baron Wakehurst of Ardingly in 1934, married Lady Louise de Vere Beauclerk, the eldest daughter of the tenth Duke of St Albans in 1890. *Philadelphus* 'Beauclerk' was actually raised by the Hon Lewis Palmer, who became a member of the Loder family — it is a most attractive mock orange. He lived at Headbourne Worthy Grange in Hampshire, where he also raised the *Agapanthus* 'Headbourne Hybrids'.

But to return to Wakehurst Place: Gerald Loder, with his head gardener, Alfred Coates, was to develop one of Britain's great gardens, a plantsman's garden, particularly of trees and shrubs. His principle interests were rhododendrons, conifers and plants of the southern hemisphere, particularly New Zealand. At Leonardslee, Gerald's brother Edmund became renowned for his development of new hybrid rhododendrons, but at Wakehurst Gerald Loder, concentrated on the natural species. 'Why must they interfere?', was Gerald's attitude to hybridisation, and a birthday gift of a specimen hybrid really became a problem — his solution was to find a site that suited the plant, but where it would receive little attention from visitors!

On the death of Gerald Loder the ownership, eventually, passed into the hands of Sir Henry Price who spent countless thousands of pounds on the restoration of the mansion. After his death the estate passed to the National Trust, along with a substantial endowment, and subsequently became a satellite garden for the Royal Botanic Gardens, Kew.

Today the grounds hold special collections of birch, willow and poplars, and of course rhododendrons. The Heath garden is best described as a 'plantsman's paradise' and much of Loder's original concepts are preserved to this day. Plants associated with the gardens include *Viburnum tinus* 'Eve Price', which has carmine buds opening to pink-tinged flowers; *Magnolia* 'Wakehurst', a hybrid of *M campbellii* — a magnificent tree for a very large garden and for patient people, for it does not generally flower until the tree is twenty to thirty years old; *Pieris formosa* 'Henry Price'; and *Pieris formosa var forrestii* 'Wakehurst' which has vivid red young foliage contrasting with its glistening white panicles of slightly fragrant flowers.

Of course Kew itself has also been responsible for introducing plants into our own gardens, including the two dwarf growing brooms, *Cytisus kewensis* and *C beanii*. A W Anderson, from New Zealand, relates in his book *The Coming of the Flowers* how Mr W Dallimore of Kew had told the following story: 'In 1891 three seedling hybrid brooms were noticed at Kew, and were removed to the nursery until stock of them had been propagated. One was named *C x kewensis*, and another was called *C x beanii*, for Mr W J Bean, who was curator at Kew, and the author of the classic book, *Trees and Shrubs Hardy in the British Isles*. One day it was reported that Mr Bean remarked that he wondered why his name

Cytisus beanii, named after one of the curators of the Royal Botanic Gardens.

The Temperate House at Kew in 1892, with the proposed new wing.

35

Helianthemum 'Wisley Pink'.

Helianthemum 'Wisley Pink'

had been given to the poor washy thing, and would not have minded if it had been the third one of the seedlings, wheron the offending plant disappeared and his name was transferred to the plant with glowing yellow florets.'

Another plant raised at Kew Gardens is *Primula x kewensis*, which first appeared as a natural hybrid, raised from seed of *Primula floribunda* in 1900. The other parent was *P verticillata* which was growing in the same glasshouse at the same time. To begin with the flowers proved to be sterile, but in 1905 a single fertile inflorescence occurred at the famous Veitch nurseries. From that seed was raised the giant-flowered fertile form which today we gardeners know as *Primula x kewensis*.

Over many years there has been rivalry between those trained at Kew and those trained at Wisley, the gardens of the Royal Horticultural Society in Surrey.

The story of Wisley starts with George Ferguson Wilson, the managing director of Price's Patent Candle Company who developed his interest in gardening at Weybridge. The *Journal of Horticulture and Cottage Gardener* wrote of him in 1876: 'Mr Wilson's pretty place, Heatherbank, is, as all the gardening world knows, the home of everything that is rare and beautiful amongst herbaceous plants and lilies, and the marvellous manner in which they grow here reflects the utmost credit on his skill as a cultivator.'

Some time later he acquired about sixty acres of land a few miles away at Wisley, where he developed an informal garden in a woodland clearing. Wilson died in 1902, having been a good friend of the Royal Horticultural Society in his lifetime. He had been their treasurer for many years and was also generous to them in other ways. Wisley was then bought by Sir Thomas Hanbury and in 1903 was given by him, in trust, to the Royal Horticultural Society. Over the past ninety years the site has expanded to almost 200 acres, and its horticultural facilities have developed so that it is both a plantsman's garden and a trial ground for flowers and vegetables — a garden known throughout the gardening world. Many plants, particularly rhododendrons and azaleas, have originated from these gardens but few bear its name, although Helianthemum 'Wisley Pink' and *H* 'Wisley Primrose' do.

The Horticultural Society, and later the Royal Horticultural Society, have sent people to collect plants from distant parts since they first had an arrangement with John Reeves in 1817, such links continuing to the days of David Douglas, and since then they have contributed to the costs of other expeditions.

It is difficult to know where to include Ellen Willmott and her famous garden at Warley place in Essex, for she influenced so many areas of plant development. I well remember, at the age of about twelve or thirteen growing *Aethionema* 'Warley Rose' in my father's small nursery in Ilkley, and having a great affection for it. Perhaps this is the right place, following on from Wisley, for she was one of its original three trustees.

She was born in 1858 into wealth and good fortune, and trained to live like a lady, with a deep understanding of music and the arts. In 1875, the family — father, mother, Ellen and her sister — moved to Warley Place, not far from Brentwood in Essex, and it was there that her love of gardening grew, and from there it extended into many other places and forms.

Miss Willmott engaged James Backhouse & Son of York, the famous nurserymen and landscape gardeners, to construct a large rock garden with deep rocky gorges, eventually opening out onto a beautiful water garden. A variety of soils was used to ensure that the needs of all her plants were as fully met as possible, and among the boulders, carefully hidden away, was a glass-roofed cave to house a specialist collection of ferns! Her choice was often enriched by plants whose seeds had been brought home by such famous plant collectors as E H Wilson and Reginald Farrer.

In 1897, when the Royal Horticultural Society instituted the Victoria Medal of Honour, the only two lady recipients were Gertrude Jekyll and Ellen Willmott, such was the mark that she had already made on horticulture. However, one of her greatest works was still to come, the publication of her famous and scholarly work *The Genus Rosa*. It was illustrated by Alfred Parson RA, who contributed no less than 154 paintings, and today it is a collectors' item.

Viola 'Jackanapes', named to commemorate Gertrude Jekyll's pet monkey.

Miss Ellen Willmott VMH, from
a pastel drawing by Signora
Mantovani Gutti in the
Garden of 1907.

Pulmonaria 'Munstead Blue'

It has been said that her skill as a cultivator, and something of her vanity, is to be seen in the great number of plants named after her. Perhaps some of the best known are *Scabiosa caucasica* 'Miss Willmott'; *Rosa willmottiae*; *Epimedium x warleyense*; *Campanula warleyensis*, a lovely double blue bell flower for the rock garden; and *Ceratostigma willmottianum* — this last-named plant was found by Ernest Wilson in the Min River Valley of West Szechan, China, in 1908. Miss Willmott received some of the seed he sent home and managed to raise two plants from it. It is from these that all the plants in cultivation have been derived. This is a most useful late-flowering shrub with clusters of plumbago-blue flowers from the end of July to the end of October, a period when most shrubs have finished flowering.

The other lady recipient of the VMH, Gertrude Jekyll, who was born in 1843, is today remembered as an artist, author, garden designer and by the plants which bear the prefix 'Munstead'.

Gertrude Jekyll first met William Robinson in 1875 and liked his style of garden design, creating the informal landscape which incorporated woodland and water features. Nearer to the house she reverted to the more intimate style of the cottage garden. It was their garden designs which brought the herbaceous plants to the forefront. As with Miss Willmott, these gardens were designed for plants, but design involving careful use of colour and texture was very important to them. Indeed Gertrude Jekyll once wrote:

'I am strongly of the opinion that the possession of a quantity of plants, however good the plants may be themselves and however ample their number, does not make a garden; it only makes a collection . . . the duty we owe to our gardens and to our own bettering in gardens is so to use the plants that they shall form beautiful pictures; and that while delighting our eyes, they should be always training those eyes to a more exalted criticism . . . in the way it is done lies the whole difference between commonplace gardening and gardening that may rightly claim to rank as fine art'.

She also wrote: 'I have learnt much from the little cottage gardens that help to make our English wayside the prettiest in the temperate world. One can hardly go into the smallest cottage garden without learning or observing something new.'

Miss Jekyll is also remembered because of the harmonious way she and Edwin Lutyens worked together on so many houses, he as architect, she designing a garden, including at her own house Munstead Wood, after which a number of plants are called. Today there are still many examples of their joint work; unfortunately, though, some of the planting detail has been lost in a lot of them.

Her books, now classics, include *Wall and Water Gardens*, *Colour in the Flower Garden*, and *Children and Gardens*, a gardening book written for children. Among her plants we remember *Pulmonaria* 'Munstead Blue', *Sedum telephium* 'Munstead Variety', and *Lavendula spica* 'Munstead Dwarf'.

5.

For Love of Roses

Antonia Ridge, the writer of a fascinating story of the Meilland family who were intimately involved with the raising and protecting of the rose which we now know as 'Peace', used the words which head this section, and they are such an eloquent description of the relationship many of our rose breeders had with the conception and rearing of their 'children'.

We will return to the Meilland family later, but for the moment let us go back to the late 1860s when in Allendale, in Northumberland, Thomas Harkness started in business as a master tailor. His two sons, Robert and John were set to follow in his footsteps, but that was not their idea. They had seen their cousins enjoying life on a neighbouring farm and they decided they would also like a life with plants — but how could they persuade their father that there was 'brass' in it! 'I know', said Robert, 'we'll each put two pence from our pocket money, buy wallflower seed and sell the plants.' The season was kind, the results good, and there was a return of forty shillings on their fourpence! They then wrote a pamphlet, *How to make two pounds out of fourpence*, and sold that too!

In 1879 the Harkness family left Allendale and moved to Leeming Bar, not far from the market town of Bedale in North Yorkshire. As 'Harkness & Sons' — the name honouring their father, who gave them financial help, — they soon made their mark. They exhibited their dahlias and gladioli at flower shows all over the north of England — and when they won they sent a telegram back to Leeming Bar, a signal to fly the Union Jack at the nursery! In the autumn of 1882, for the first time, we find them selling roses: '12 fine plants, carriage paid, 10s 6d; or 24 for £1.' That same year they exhibited at the Crystal Palace but very much felt that 'the judges were biased in favour of the southern nurserymen'. However they were not beaten for long, for in 1887 at the National Rose Society's Summer Show in London, to the amazement of everyone, they carried away the premier trophy, the championship. Dean Hole, for many years president of the NRS, said to them afterwards, 'Well, boys, you've done it, but you'll never do it again. The season has been all in your favour for once, and against the rest of us.' They did not take this statement lightly, and recognised some truth in it. If they wanted continued success they would have to consider moving south.

E B Lindsell, an amateur champion of the rose world, and solicitor, lived in Hitchin, Hertfordshire. He also acted as land agent for the local squire and it was to him that approaches were made. And so from Michaelmas 1892 they leased

'Mrs Harkness', introduced in 1893.

39

Above: 'Ena Harkness', a rose that has stood the test of time, and has delighted thousands of rose lovers over the years.

Right: This picture of the Harkness family taken in 1895 includes Gladys Harkness with her siblings, the baby Etta, Elsie is on the right with Verney Leigh (father of Jack and Peter Harkness) in his sailor suit. 'Gladys Harkness' was a pink rose which was raised by Dixon and Son and popular for several years; Elsie's name was given to a pink sidalcea 'Elsie Heugh' and 'V L Harkness' was a white chrysanthemum.

the Rose Field at Charlton near Hitchin. 1893 saw the introduction of their first rose, 'Mrs Harkness', a hybrid perpetual.

In those early days they tried to manage the new enterprise from a distance, but it did not work. In 1895 they again discussed their future and the outcome was that one of them should move to Hitchin to live. But who? They decided to toss a coin, and Robert lost! It was agreed that Robert should take every other one of the dormant budded stocks, and he and his family made what at that time was a very long journey south.

With 1914 came many problems and by 1918 all that was left of the enterprise was its name and goodwill. It was into this state of affairs that William (Bill) Harkness came, even before he was 'demobbed'. He purchased the goodwill, and with it the mailing list of customers, and bought up an already grown rose crop that another grower had been unable to sell. It was insufficient to support himself, wife and family, so he worked on the holding in the daytime and at night he became the landlord of the Raven Inn at Hexton, near Hitchin. Within four years he had done well enough that he was able to move back to Hitchin. However, it was not until 1932 that the name Harkness could be engraved again on the championship trophy.

Back up in the north of England, J Harkness & Son were busy raising new varieties of lupins, and gaining Awards of Merit for them at the Royal Horticultural Society. Unfortunately John Harkness died in 1933 and his nursery did not survive the Second World War.

However, in 1936, William moved his business to the present site north-east of Hitchin. By sheer hard work, and insistence on high quality and integrity, he built a very successful business. The year 1939 saw the largest and best crop of all, but alas Hitler prevented it being sold — most of the roses were burnt! Throughout the war only a nucleus of plants could be saved for happier times, their place being taken by carrots, onions and brussels sprouts.

Even in the midst of war, 1942 was a bright year. Albert Norman, a Hatton Garden diamond setter and amateur rose breeder, who eventually became president of the National Rose society, sent some of his seedlings to Hitchin 'to see if you think they are any good'. Two certainly were! These were a crimson hybrid tea and a crimson floribunda. Mr Norman wanted the best one to be named after W E Harkness, but William Harkness asked him to name it after his wife instead, and so the hybrid tea rose became 'Ena Harkness', one of the best-loved roses of all time. The floribunda became 'Frensham', named after a village near Farnham, in Surrey, not far from where Albert Norman lived.

In 1959 William died, and it was Jack Harkness who took over the management of the company, and who quickly started into rose breeding, gaining much help from both Pat Dickson and Sam McGredy. Brother Peter also joined him in the business. Two of our well-known roses are named after Peter and Margaret's

Bottom: 'Anne Harkness', named after Anne, Rosemary's sister, the daughter of Peter and Margaret Harkness.

Below: Rosemary Harkness toasts 'her' rose at the Chelsea Flower Show.

Top: Ena Harkness, 'a lovely lady'.

Above: 'Wedding Day' flowered for the first time on the wedding anniversary of Sir Frederick and Lady Stern.

Rose 'Wedding Day'

daughters, 'Anne Harkness' and 'Rosemary Harkness'.

Jack and Peter are grandsons of John Harkness, their father being Verney Leigh who kept out of rose growing, and joined the Civil Service instead. 'Elizabeth Harkness' is the daughter of Jack and Betty Harkness, and their two sons, Robert and Philip, now manage the company. Jack, however, until recently planned breeding programmes from his home at Southwold in Suffolk.

We have mentioned the roses, but what do we know of the ladies in the Harkness dynasty? 'Mrs Harkness', introduced in 1893, and described as a 'light coloured hybrid perpetual rose', was the wife of our master tailor, way back in Allendale. 'Gladys Harkness', introduced in 1900, was the elder daughter of John Harkness. 'Marion Harkness', Verney's second wife, was named to mark the centenary of the firm in 1979.

However, it is perhaps right that we should devote most space to Ena Harkness. Ena was born Ena Everest in Portsmouth. When she was a young woman, her father invited Bill Harkness to his home to advise him about restoring the rose garden. Ena saw this attractive young man from an upstairs window, and rushed down to see who the visitor was. On knowing that Bill Harkness had a wife and family, she dismissed him from her mind. However, ten years later Bill's wife died, and subsequently Bill and Ena married. Years later she expressed it in these words: 'I must have had it in my subconscious that he was the man I was going to marry'.

Her love of flower gardening made her anxious to develop her love of roses in a practical way, but the war intervened. During that period when they could only grow a few roses it was Ena, along with one other member of the nursery staff, who cared for them with thoroughness. And it was in her honour that Albert Norman's rose was named. Ena Harkness served as a member of the council of the Royal National Rose Society, also becoming an international demonstrator and lecturer in floral art. At her funeral in February 1990 it was said of her 'If Ena had a failing it was that she was so thoughtful and considerate for others, that she could be difficult to help; she didn't consider her own needs but was always performing kindnesses.' Ena Harkness; — a beautiful rose and obviously a lovely lady.

Another romantic story is that of the rose 'Wedding Day', a climber with white to pink flowers, said to have been the result of a cross between *R sinowilsonii* and *R moyesii*. Its raiser was the well-known plantsman Sir Frederick Stern, and as it flowered for the first time on the wedding anniversary of Sir Frederick and Lady Stern he named it 'Wedding Day'.

Rosa 'Wolley-Dod' is a shrub rose with clear rose-pink blooms which contrast with the grey-green downy foliage in early summer, and which in September produces very large, bristly crimson heps. The Rev J F Hurt married a Miss Wolley, and on their marriage he assumed her surname. They had only one son,

Rose 'Wolley-Dod'.

Rose 'Felicité et Perpetué'

Charles, and when he married the grand-daughter of Mr R C Dod of Edge Hall in Cheshire he went to live at that residence and became known as Wolley Dod! He was actually the Rev Charles Wolley-Dod, who had an extensive interest in both gardening and botanical matters. A man before his time?

Two saints, Perpetua and Felicitas, were martyred in Carthage in AD 203 by being thrown to the beasts in the arena. Felicitas was the slave of Perpetua, who was married to a Roman patrician. There is a story, however, that Felicitas need not have died, but so deep was her attachment to her mistress that she chose to share her fate.

In *A Rose Odyssey* the author J H Nicholas recalls that Jacques, the head gardener of the park of Neuilly, near Paris had set aside a rose which he would name to commemorate 'a bundle from heaven' which his wife was expecting. However, his wife gave birth to twin girls. He had only one rose, so he gave it both names, Felicité and Perpetué. 'Felicité et Perpetué' is a beautiful climber with white rosette-style flowers, appropriately with touches of red upon them. It was introduced in 1927.

I mentioned at the beginning of this chapter the book by Antonia Ridge dedicated to the story of the Meilland family, but I am also grateful for the following facts, which are only a minute part of an account of the Meilland story in Jack Harkness's superb book *The Makers of Heavenly Roses*.

Antoine Meilland was born in 1884 at Chamboeuf, in France, one of four children. His mother, Jeanne, known as Jenny, brought them up well in spite of a lack of money and only having one hand, the lost one being replaced by an iron hook.

As a young lad of twelve he had already been influenced by the widow of a local schoolmaster. Mme Mivière had a garden which the young Antoine admired, particularly the roses! She taught him how to bud a rose, and on his next visit into town with his mother he took all his savings and invested them in a budding knife — even at that early age he told his parents that he wanted to be a rose grower. His father tried to dissuade him, but his mind was made up, and with assistance from Mme Mivière he wrote to Francis Dubreuil, a Lyon rose grower, seeking work. He was told to get work nearer to home, and then when sixteen years old to apply again. Both these things he did, and so learned the skills he had desired for so long. Francis Dubreuil had already introduced some roses bred by his late father-in-law, Joseph Rambaux, among them 'Perle d'Or', a china rose with miniature blooms of a light pink and yellow colour — it is still grown today, although introduced in 1884. As Antoine's love of roses grew, so did his love for Claudia, his employer's daughter, and after being there nine years he asked that he might marry her.

In 1912 Francis Meilland was born, but soon war came to France and Antoine had to leave the nursery to fight the Germans. Back at the nursery Claudia had to start growing vegetables, and during this period Francis Dubreuil died.

It wasn't until 1919 that they were re-united and once again grew the roses that they loved. the first year, however, the crop was wiped out by a root pest and Antoine's interest in rose-breeding had to be temporarily abandoned.

Soon, however, they were able to sell the old nursery and move to a new site which gave them greater opportunities for success. By now their son, young Francis, was also keen to join the business.

In 1929 Antoine and Francis were invited, along with other rose growers and their sons, to see the new roses of Charles Mallerin, an engineer turned rose-breeder. This event made a great impression on the young Francis, and that very same summer he began breeding roses — he had a great heritage behind him, right back to great-grandfather, Joseph Rambaux. His mother Claudia gave him every encouragement, especially in those days when nothing seemed to succeed, and Charles Mallerin willingly gave him information and advice; and he also introduced him to Mr Pyle, of the Conard-Pyle Company of America.

Hardly had signs of success started germinating when Antoine and Francis suffered a grievous loss when Claudia died in her early forties. Fortunately Grand-mère Jenny took control of the situation, and sent the bereaved husband and son to a hotel in Antibes for a holiday to ease their mourning. Whilst there they decided to call upon one of their customers, one they had never met, Francesco Paolino, an Italian immigrant. He also had known hard times and immediately the two were moved from their hotel room and into the Paolino family home. Young Francis met young Louisette Paolino and seven years later they were married.

In 1935 Francis went to America to see what there was to learn from such a progressive country. He came back with three important ideas in his mind: the necessity of a good catalogue with coloured illustrations, the need to mechanise, and the use of cool storage to keep plants in good condition for sale. The following year Meilland's catalogue was in colour!

His first successful variety of rose was introduced in America in 1937 by Conard-Pyle. Robert Pyle chose the name 'Golden State' which linked with the international exhibition in San Francisco, and its success was assured. The royalties were promptly spent on a cool store!

That same year that Francis had gone to America, on the 15th June 1935 some roses were pollinated — the actual parentage is not certain — and from one of the seeds a weak seedling arose. A few eyes were budded in 1936 and in October of that year one of them shot away and produced a flower. Its vigour, its fine dark foliage and its wonderful large flowers in shades of delicate yellow and pink, declared it to be an outstanding Hybrid Tea, perhaps the best that the world had ever seen!

In 1939 Francis and Louisette married, and during that summer Francis sent eyes of his special rose to America, Germany and Italy. Within weeks France was

Rose 'Felicité et Perpetué', a beautiful rose with a fascinating story.

45

once again at war with Germany — again it was vegetables, not roses. A friend in the United States consulate in Lyon telephoned Francis to say that the consul was leaving by air for the United States and was willing to take a small package with him. Within two hours a packet was delivered to him and in it was some more propagating material of that special rose, just in case the previous consignment, of which Francis had heard nothing, had gone astray.

In 1943, Grandmère Jenny died, although it wasn't until several years later that a rose was introduced that commemorated her great contribution to the rose story.

But during this period what was happening to Francis's special rose? In France it was introduced as 'Mme A Meilland', in memory of his mother, Claudia; in Germany it became known as 'Gloria Dei', and in Italy as 'Gioia'. In America, unknown to the Meillands, Robert Pyle had sought the help of his colleagues in rose growing, and had it tested in various parts of the United States. In every case it had received glowing reports, and the American Rose Society agreed for it to be named at the Pacific Rose Society's exhibition in Pasadena on Sunday the 29th April 1945 — that date was fixed months in advance. The name was 'Peace' — and on that very day Berlin fell! Antonia Ridge tells us that 'two white doves were set free and soared high into the blue Californian sky'.

Rose 'Peace' — a name to influence men's thoughts towards everlasting peace.

46

Shortly afterwards, at a meeting of delegates of the United Nations, in San Francisco, in each delegate's room was a flower of 'Peace', and with it a message: 'This is the Peace rose which was christened at the Pacific Rose Society Convention in Pasadena on the day Berlin fell. We hope the Peace rose will influence men's thought for everlasting world peace.'

It is easy to dwell on the sombre things of life, but the Germans, now our partners in Europe, have produced some wonderful roses. One of the best remembered of our old roses is 'Frau Karl Druschki' which is said to have first flowered in its raiser's garden in 1899. It was raised by Peter Lambert of Trier by crossing 'Merveille de Lyon' with 'Mme Caroline Testout'. He exhibited it at a rose show in Berlin, where it won the title of best new rose of the year, but with the obligation that it be named to commemorate the wife of the president of the society, hence the name 'Frau Karl Druschki'. It is still available from nurseries today, known for its purity of whiteness and form.

Another old rose, of a very different form, was discovered growing in a Swiss village — in Mauborget. The story goes that although the village was destroyed by fire, an outlying chalet survived, and with it this charming little rose. When the village was rebuilt the rose was gradually given from one neighbour to another. Major Roulet, of the Swiss Army, visited the village towards the end of the First World War and took an instant liking to the little flower. From Major Roulet it was passed to the Geneva alpine specialist Henri Correvon, and so to the rest of us. It usually only grows to a height of three or four inches, carrying delightful, small, pink, perfect roses. It is a good choice for a small trough or on a low wall.

To some people, roses are just roses! To others they must be categorised into a selection of groupings, some of which have changed their names and definitions as the years have passed by. Some people like the perfect shape of a Hybrid Tea whilst others prefer an old-fashioned shrub rose with a rich, almost overpowering scent. For those who look for a flower similar to our wild rose, but of a completely different colour, perhaps *Rosa xanthina* 'Canary Bird' is for them. It was introduced in 1946 by John Russell of L R Russell Ltd of Windlesham in Surrey. Its colour exactly matches canary-yellow on the RHS colour chart, so he chose the name 'Canary'. It was given an immediate Award of Merit by the RHS committee, but they pointed out that as there was already a rose of that name a new name was needed. And so *R x* 'Canary Bird' came into being.

As in all fields of business, so in rose growing, sponsorship has become important, and quite sizeable amounts are paid to have a quality rose named after your company, which the sponsor and the rose breeder hope will stay to the forefront in popularity. Some achieve this, others fade away more quickly!

One that has certainly stood the test of time is 'Caroline Testout', which we mentioned a few sentences ago. Mme Testout was a Parisian couturier, a lady with an eye for business, who approached Joseph Pernet-Ducher, seeing the

Top: Rose 'City of Bradford', used to promote this Yorkshire city.

Above: Rose 'Hand in Hand', named to celebrate 125 years of NCH — Action for Children.

Rose 'Fellowship'

Above: In its name the rose 'Fellowship' conveys one of the most important qualities of the worldwide Rotary movement.

Opposite Page Left: The rose 'Elizabeth of Glamis' reminds us of Queen Elizabeth the Queen Mother.

Opposite Page Top Right: Rose 'Mrs Sam McGredy'. It was Sam McGredy III who named the rose after his mother.

Opposite Page Bottom Right: Rose 'Queen Elizabeth', named in honour of Queen Elizabeth II.

concept of a rose bearing her name as an advertisement for her business. The chosen rose, with flowers of satiny-pink, was introduced in her London salon in the spring of 1890. Her rose still lives on long after the death of a lady who, if not the first, was one of the earliest to see the value of plants in this way. Within the last twenty years we have seen roses bearing the names of such products as Bonsoir (shirts), Basildon Bond (writing paper), Peaudouce (disposable nappies), and such institutions as *International Herald Tribune* (newspaper), and Savoy Hotel. Other names have appeared, as towns and cities have seen this as a way of promoting their image — so we have 'City of Bradford', 'Southampton', 'City of London', 'Pride of Maldon', and 'Letchworth Garden City'. Charities have also worked with rose breeders and their names have also become linked with a special rose, the charity often gaining some financial benefit during the early years of the rose's life. Examples of this are 'Samaritan', 'Guiding Spirit' (for the world Guide movement), 'Rosy Future' (a name chosen in a competition, a descriptive name for the Cardinal Hume Centre which helps young people who are at risk), 'Fellowship' (conveying one of the most important qualities of the worldwide Rotary movement and also raising funds for Rotary foundation, the charity which offers help throughout the world), and 'High Hopes' (for Oxfam). Other people see the naming of a rose as a way of saying thank you or of publicly showing one's affection for another — 'Emily Louise' in memory of a little girl who was tragically drowned in the *Herald of Free Enterprise* ferry disaster, or on a more happy note 'Pat James' to celebrate the golden wedding of Pat and Gordon James, a way of thanking her for many years of happiness, and also for her untiring work for charity.

I began this look at roses with two famous 'rose families' and conclude with another family that will always be linked with roses: the name of McGredy. Samuel McGredy was born in 1828, and after a career in 'private service' in which he became a head gardener, he opened his own nursery just outside Portadown in County Armagh in 1880. The land, ten acres of it, was leased, but it was fertile and on it he grew show pansies, very popular plants in those days. There is no mention of roses in those early days, but nevertheless when he died in 1903 he left a good business and a keen, enthusiastic son, Samuel. During those last years of the nineteenth century, however, they did begin to deal in roses and probably about 1895 started breeding them in a very modest way. In 1905 — nothing comes quickly in rose breeding — McGredy exhibited for the first time at London and, amazingly, he gained the gold medal of the National Rose Society with his rose 'Countess of Gosford'. Sam McGredy II was never at a loss for words either in describing the virtues of his new roses, or even his remedy for rose mildew! He described his 1912 novelty 'British Queen' as the 'finest white rose in existence', and his 1914 'Florence Forrester' he said was 'the grandest of all whites'. In 1921 he was awarded the National Rose Society's Dean Hole

Opposite Page Bottom: *Azalea Hinode-giri*, one of E H Wilson's famous fifty varieties.

Opposite Page Middle & Top: Jelena de Belder and **(above)** the plant which was her wedding present, *Hamamelis x intermedia* 'Jelena'.

Rose 'Mrs Sam McGredy'

Medal, and at this time was raising 17,000 seedlings a year — a far cry from the 300 seedlings a year they grew a quarter of a century earlier.

Sadly Samuel McGredy II died suddenly in 1926. Some of his finest roses were still to be introduced and the world of roses had lost one of its best-loved characters — an appreciation of him in the *Rose Annual* described him as 'one of the finest, most straightforward and conscientious Rosarians that ever walked'. Samuel McGredy III was only twenty-nine years old when his father died, but he quickly gathered up the reins. He had married Ruth Darragh and they had three children who were all to make their mark on the world of roses. It was Sam III who started the tradition of 'McGredy roses', ones named after members of the family, and so we find in 1927 the first of these, 'Margaret McGredy', named after his mother, followed by 'Mrs Sam McGredy' named after his wife.

In between these introductions, in November 1934, Sam III also died suddenly when only thirty-eight years old — at that time Sam IV was only two years old. It was indeed a calamity. Sam III's sister had married a man called Walter Johnston, and although he was no rose breeder it was he more than anybody who kept the nursery together, particularly through the war years.

After a good schooling and a mixture of training, Sam IV came 'home' to the nursery at Portadown. What he did not know about roses or rose breeding he soon set about learning, gaining information from all the best growers and breeders in Europe and America. He sowed his first crop of rose seed in 1955 and later that year had 20,000 seedlings from which to select! The breeding instinct was in this man as it had been in his father and grandfather before him — McGredy's were on their way back up to the top. His first success was 'Salute', in 1958, followed the next year by 'Orangeade', a gold medal-winning floribunda. Over the years many others have followed, including such well-loved varieties as 'Piccadilly', 'Mischief', and 'Elizabeth of Glamis' — 'Mischief' was named after a little dog, and 'Elizabeth of Glamis' was virtually by royal appointment, for the Queen Mother gave her permission; it has won many top awards including the President's International Trophy, and deservedly so.

In 1972 Sam IV moved away from Northern Ireland to New Zealand, to carry on his rose breeding and build a new life away from the troubles of his own land. Still his roses come to this and other countries, and here dedicated amateur and professional breeders continue to work to provide us with beautiful roses, blooms to admire on a lovely summer's day.

Finally another royal rose, raised by Dr W E Lammerts, an American, from 'Charlotte Armstrong' x 'Floradora', and introduced by Germains Nursery at Los Angeles, in 1954. Harry Wheatcroft saw the rose under trial and it is suggested that he said that it be named after Queen Elizabeth II as she was just beginning her reign.

6.
Trees and Shrubs

About 1825, Monsieur Mortier, a Ghent nurseryman had the idea of crossing the early-flowering varieties of azalea, which were susceptible to frost damage, with the pollen of later flowering varieties — the experiment succeeded. Not only were flowers with a later flowering tendency secured, but they also had better form, more varied colour and a more pleasing fragrance. Originally they were known as *Azalea mortierana* before becoming better known as Ghent azaleas. They were raised from various crosses using *Rhododendron viscosum*, *nudiflorum*, *luteum* and *calendulaceum*.

The evergreen and semi-evergreen azaleas came from Japan. The famous plant collector E H Wilson chose fifty different varieties from a nursery on Mount Kurume and sent them to the Arnold Arboretum in America. From there, through the generosity of Dr Sargent, a collection of them was sent to England where several have become popular, including the clear pink flowered 'Hino-mayo', and the bright crimson 'Hinode-giri'.

During the summer of 1954 a young Yugoslavian student gardener came to Belgium. She had previously worked in Germany and Holland, but now she had arrived at the Van Geert nursery which had been taken over by the two de Belder brothers. It was full of interesting trees and shrubs, and Robert de Belder showed her a row of witch hazels, unnamed, but selected seedlings, which had been chosen by the former director of the nursery, Mr Kort. They were still crowded together in their original lines and in urgent need of transplanting. Jelena, our student gardener, had seen *hamamelis* rooted from cuttings in the famous German nursery of Tim & Co, and decided it would be safer to propagate these seedlings rather than attempting to transplant them at this stage. Robert, however, was sceptical, but said that if the cuttings succeeded he would name the best form after her.

After only three meetings Robert and Jelena decided to marry. It had been love at first sight and together they went back to Yugoslavia for the wedding.

When they arrived back in Belgium in January 1955 they were delighted to find that a few cuttings had rooted and were flowering. Robert took some branches over to London, to the Royal Horticultural Society's show, and this new form was given an award of merit — and of course the name 'Jelena'. As Jelena

Hamamelis 'Jelena'

herself said, in a letter to me, 'It was a wedding present'.

The shrub has a spreading habit with yellow flowers, suffused with a rich coppery-red. The foliage also gives good autumn colours of orange, red and scarlet. Hillier's *Manual of Trees and Shrubs*, one of gardening's great books, states, 'named after a great gardener, Jelena de Belder' — a nice compliment.

Some plants have started their life in research stations, some in nurseries or private gardens, but others have been found growing in the wild. Such a plant is *Cytisus albus* 'Andreanus', which was found growing wild in Normandy by Monsieur Edouard André. The shrub which bears his name has now been cultivated for over a century and has given great joy in many gardens with its bronze and gold blooms.

M André had a nursery at La Croix, near the village of Blire, and among some *Prunus mume* seedlings he noticed one with bronze leaves. It flowered for the first time in 1901 and was then identified as a natural hybrid between *Prunus cerasifera* 'Pissardii' and *P mume* — four years later it was introduced as *Prunus x blireiana*, and has become accepted as one of the best of the coloured-leaved flowering plums. P cerasifera 'Pissardii' is named after a Frenchman, M René Pissard, who became gardener to the Shah of Persia in 1880.

In the early days after their introduction mahonias, the Oregon Grapes, were often regarded as part of the genus *Berberis*, and therefore the plant we now know as *Mahonia aquifolium* was known as *Berberis aquifolia*. Thomas Nuttall, a Yorkshireman who emigrated to Philadelphia, and later became regarded as the father of American botany, was responsible for this change of name. He became curator of Harvard Botanic Garden and had the genus of shrub *Nuttallia* named in his honour, but he also wrote two volumes entitled *The Genera of North America Plants* in 1818. It was in this book that part of the genus *Berberis* became known as *Mahonia*, after an American nurseryman and seedsman Bernard McMahon. McMahon also lived in Philadelphia, but originally came from Ireland, having left that country for political reasons in 1796.

Two plant collectors, Lewis and Clark, had collected seed of various plants on a visit from the far west to Philadelphia, and McMahon had been entrusted with some of these. He was successful in raising a number of new plants, but had been instructed to keep them secret and not distribute them until the official account of the expedition and their descriptions had been published. For various reasons, not least the war between Britain and America, this work was delayed. Among the plants raised was the then unknown snowberry, *Symphoricarpos*, and *Berberis aquifolia*, which became *Mahonia aquifolium* in memory of Thomas Nuttall's friend, for McMahon had died two years earlier aged forty-one.

Robert Fortune, the well-known plant collector, who was brought up at Edrom in Berwickshire, and later studied at the Royal Botanic Gardens, Edinburgh, developed a friendship with Thomas Beale, who had a garden in Shanghai; in his

Opposite Page Top: Monsieur Edouard André.

Opposite Page Bottom: *Cytisus albus* 'Andreanus'.

honour he named a most beautiful winter-flowering plant, *Berberis bealei*, or as we now know it *Mahonia bealei*. How he procured it was set down in a letter he wrote to the *Gardeners' Chronicle* from China. He told how, with his Chinese coolie, he had been collecting tea seeds on a small hill near the town of Tun-che, when he saw a very fine specimen of the funereal cypress, *Cupressus funebris*. He soon discovered that it was in a garden enclosed by a high wall. Together they walked round the walls until they came to a little cottage, which served as a lodge, and coolly walked into the garden! They soon found themselves in the middle of the dilapidated garden of a ruined mansion. The cypress was about fifty feet high, and they collected ripe seed from it. Whilst on their way out of the garden, Fortune noticed an extraordinary plant in a secluded corner. He discovered it was a very fine evergreen berberis, of the mahonia section, with coarse pinnate leaves. He described how each leaflet was nearly as large as the leaf of an English holly, spiny and of a fine, dark, shining green colour. It was almost eight feet high, much branched, and far surpassed in beauty all the known species of mahonia — indeed it had only one fault, it was too large to move and bring away! However, Fortune took a leaf, and marked the spot where the plant grew, thinking he would get some cuttings on his return journey to base.

Robert Fortune sought the help of his servants to find some young plants of

Above Left: *Mahonia bealei*, named after Robert Fortune's friend, Thomas Beale.

Above: *Prunus cerasifera* 'Pissardii' commemorates the Shah of Persia's gardener.

53

Above: *Buddleja* 'Lochinch'.

Top: Lochinch Castle in Scotland, home of the Earl of Stair.

Buddleja davidii

the mahonia, believing that if it was in one garden it would surely be in others, but none were found, or as Fortune later reveals, perhaps none were looked for! However, he knew that dollars had a 'potent influence', and so he called some of the family of servants together and offered a dollar if they brought him a young plant with a leaf of the same type as the one he had shown them. In less than five minutes a servant returned with such a leaf, and Fortune said to him: 'That will do, that is just the thing I want; bring me a young plant with good roots, and I shall give you the promised reward'. But still it would seem Fortune was no nearer, for the Chinese group would neither sell him a plant nor take him to see where it was. Eventually they gave way and took him to a small cottage garden, nearly overgrown with weeds. Here the beautiful shrub was growing, apparently neglected and left to bloom unseen. Again he tried to persuade them, but they were not willing to let the plant go, claiming that it had special medical qualities, giving marvellous benefit to those suffering from blows or concussion and also rheumatism — the roots being cut into small pieces and boiled, and the decoction swallowed!

However, on the following day another Chinese relation came secretly and informed Fortune that he knew where the species could be procured, and that he was willing to fetch some. Again the stipulation about young plants with good roots was given, and good as his word he returned within the day and sold the plants to Fortune.

Fortune succeeded in getting them down to Shanghai in good condition — to Mr Beale's garden — and put in his footnote, 'Named in compliment to my friend Mr Beale of Shanghae, in whose garden many of my finest plants have been preserved.' We tend to think of plant movement always being from China and Japan to Britain or America, but comment is made that Beale had a plant of the American *Magnolia grandiflora*!

Many people think of buddleias as plants with long racemes of purple flowers, often attracting large numbers of butterflies. These are the varieties of *Buddleja davidii* (*davidii* celebrates Armand David, a missionary). But there are some interesting crosses which have been achieved using this as one of the parents.

The Kennedys received their first charter of lands in Galloway from the king in the middle of the fourteenth century; John, Lord Kennedy, was appointed keeper of the Manor Place and Loch of Inch in 1482. Although Castle Kennedy was known to have been standing in 1482, it was burnt down in 1716, and today stands as a ruin. Lochinch Castle was built in 1867 and today is the family home of the Earl of Stair. Within the grounds is a monkey puzzle avenue, reputed to be one of the longest in the country and until the gales of 1963 it was also one of the finest. The origin of *Buddleja* 'Lochinch' is not known, but it is from this garden that it takes its name. It is a medium-sized shrub, with greyish foliage and scented flowers of violet blue with a deep orange eye.

Fuchsia riccartonii

Mr W van de Weyer lived at Sledmere House at Corfe Castle in Dorset during the early years of this century and during that period tried to persuade *Buddleja davidii var magnifica* and *B globosa* to flower simultaneously so that he might cross them. Unfortunately with the outbreak of the First World War he had to join the army, but on one of his weekend leaves he found to his great delight two ball-shaped flowers on a *Buddleja globosa*. He crossed one with a *B davidii var magnifica*, the other with *B madagascariensis*. When he came home on leave from France he saw his plants in flower. *B globosa* normally flowers in May, whilst the others are autumn flowering. The seedlings were all autumn flowering, the flowers were ball-like but with greyish-white heads, tinted with violet, except for one which had ball-shaped spikes of yellowish-white, and all were fragrant. Weyer collected seed from these, although in some cases the plants were almost infertile. The second generation seedlings were also all autumn flowering but had brighter-coloured flowers. The named form has ball-shaped heads of orange yellow, often tinged with mauve, the flowers being borne in long slender panicles on the young wood in summer. Weyer was hoping for a long panicle of yellow flowers; it was not to be but the result is most interesting!

Hebe pinguifolia 'Pagei', named after a gardener in the Antipodes.

The Riccarton Estate, on the outskirts of Edinburgh, is fully recorded back to 1315 when it was given by King Robert the Bruce to his daughter, Marjory, on the occasion of her marriage to Walter the high steward.

Riccarton House, which was previously occupied by the Craigs of Riccarton, has now been demolished and the site forms part of Heriot-Watt University. Its horticultural claim to fame lies in the *Fuchsia riccartonii*, a hardy shrub which in mild districts is used as a hedge. The red calyx tube is scarcely a quarter of an inch long, but combined with the purple petals produces a most attractive flower. John Downie, the Edinburgh nurseryman (whose story is found further on in this chapter), testified that it was raised by John Young the gardener at Riccarton in the 1830s. Mr Young once said, 'I have made no money from it, but I have the satisfaction to know that I have raised something to beautify my country'. If only we could all be satisfied with such a claim!

John Downie, the Edinburgh nurseryman.

Whilst many plants have come from China and Japan, comparatively few have come to us from Australasia. One welcome plant from New Zealand is *Hebe pinguifolia* 'Pagei'. It commemorates Edward Page, a native of Sussex who emigrated to New Zealand in 1912. He worked in Dunedin Botanic Garden and later as superintendent of the grounds to the Otago Hospital and Charitable Aid Board. *Hebe* 'Pagei' was received at the Royal Botanic Gardens Kew in 1925 from Dunedin, although it had previously been grown as *Veronica* 'Pageana' (many of the *Hebes* were previously commonly known as shrubby Veronicas) in the garden of Mr Haddon at Portlock in Somerset. It received a preliminary commendation when displayed at Chelsea Show in 1947, before receiving an Award of Merit in 1958.

'Leyland's Cypress'

There are many attractive escallonias, and a large number of the hybrids were selected at the Slieve Donard nurseries, near the Mountains of Mourne in Ireland, examples being 'Donard Seedling' and 'Pride of Donard'. One other escallonia, said to be a seedling of *E macrantha*, is the result of work done at Glasnevin Botanic Gardens in Dublin by Mr C F Ball. He later gave cuttings of one to Mr G N Smith of Newry, a local nurseryman who simply labelled them 'CFB'. Alas C F Ball died of wounds received in the First World War in 1915, but his memory lives on in his escallonia, which received the Award of Merit in 1926.

Some men work for immortality, others have it cast upon them by other people. William Forsyth, who was born in Old Meldrum, in Aberdeenshire in 1737, attained great respect from his horticultural contemporaries by having charge of His Majesty's garden at Chelsea and by being a founder member of the Horticultural Society, in 1804. Indeed, in 1801 John Wedgwood had written to Forsyth about the formation of such a society (John Wedgwood was the son of Josiah Wedgwood who founded the firm of potters). Forsyth was also present at the inaugural meeting in the house of Mr Hatchard, the bookseller, of Piccadilly in London.

It was Vahl who honoured Forsyth by naming the genus of spring-flowering shrubs 'Forsythia'. William Forsyth died in July 1804, only four months after that inaugural meeting which was the birth of such an important society.

A rather more modern shrub, but one that has become almost as familiar, is *X Cupressocyparis leylandii*, the popular hedging conifer. It started its life in the Welsh border country, at Leighton Hall, near Welshpool. Its origin was related in the Royal Horticultural Society's *Journal*:

'In 1888 Mr C J Leyland, at Leighton Hall, collected seeds from a tree of *Chamaecyparis nootkatensis*, which was growing near a tree of *Cupressus macrocarpa*. The seedling trees which resulted were later planted at Haggerstone Castle in Northumberland. As they developed it was noticed that six of them differed in appearance and growth from the rest, and in time it became evident that they were the result of a natural cross.

Subsequently Leighton Hall passed into the possession of Captain J M Naylor, Mr Leyland's nephew, and in 1911 seeds were collected from the other parent, *Cupressus macrocarpa*, which was growing near a tree of *Chamaecyparis nootkatensis*. Among the seedlings raised, two were noticed to differ in growth. They were planted out in due course and their development was watched with interest. In July 1925 Captain Naylor sent a branch with cones from one of the trees to the Royal Botanic Gardens at Kew, with particulars of its origin as a seedling from *Cupressus macrocarpa*.

As the tree has the fern-like sprays of foliage of *Chamaecyparis nootkatensis*, but with larger cones, the probability of a hybrid having occurred was suspected. Careful examination of the cones of the hybrid and the two possible parents revealed that not only were the cones of the Leighton Hall tree intermediate in size, but the number of scales on the cones were intermediate between those of the cones of *Cupressus macrocarpa* and *Chamaecyparis nootkatensis*.

It is interesting to record that specimens sent to Kew reveal that at least one of the earlier trees, now growing at Haggerstone, raised in 1888, from *Chamaecyparis nootkatensis*, exactly resembles in foliage and cones the tree raised in 1911 from the reciprocal cross when *Cupressus macrocarpa* was the seed parent.'

A golden form of *X Cupressocyparis leylandii* saw its birth in the garden of one of Ireland's most beautiful homes. Castlewellan's name is derived from Castlewilliam, after William Annesley, who was created Baron Annesley in 1758. Castlewellan is near Newcastle and the Mountains of Mourne, and has had a garden from as early as 1740, when a cottage or perhaps a fishing house was built near the lake. This was pulled down when the fourth earl began building the castle, but it was his brother, Hugh, who succeeded him, who started laying out the garden, bringing plants from all parts of the world, not least many conifers.

During the 1940s Mr Gerald Annesley inherited the estate and John Keown joined him as head gardener. It was the latter who noticed a seedling of *Chamaecyparis nootkatensis aurea x Cupressus macrocarpa*. When the full beauty of the tree was seen, attempts were made to graft it onto a rootstock of *Cupressus macrocarpa*, but after many attempts the grafts still did not take. One day, after the disheartened propagator had gathered up his tools, he left the apprentice to brush up the floor; the apprentice, on seeing a small number of bright yellow cuttings, gathered them up into a flowerpot of sand. Some weeks later the master propagator noticed the cuttings still looked fresh and on closer examination found they had rooted.

The plant became known as *X Cupressocyparis leylandii* 'Castlewellan' and was introduced in 1971 by Northern Ireland's Ministry of Agriculture Forestry Division.

Whilst the *leylandii* types have become increasingly popular in recent years, particularly as hedges, it was the introduction of an earlier conifer which perhaps made a greater change in the British landscape, a plant we now know and love as *Chamaecyparis lawsoniana*, and its hosts of variations.

The name of Lawson in agricultural and horticultural matters goes back over two hundred years, for it was in 1770 that the firm is thought to have commenced. The first entry in the *Edinburgh Directory* is found in 1790, when Peter Lawson is listed as a seed merchant in Blair Street. In 1818 he obtained a nursery in Grange Toll, but the address best associated with the company was No 1 George IV Bridge, Edinburgh.

The original Peter Lawson was both apprenticed and entered as a Burgess on the 5th October 1786. This was a unusual occurrence, and was specially author-

THE LAWSON NURSERIES,
EDINBURGH.

Evergreen Shrubs for Present Planting.
Rhododendrons, Ivies in Pots, &c., &c.

Hothouse, Greenhouse, and Bedding-out Plants
in great variety.

TODEA SUPERBA — several hundreds,
among which some magnificent specimens, perhaps the
finest ever imported.

CLEMATISES in POTS—a large Collection
of all the leading varieties, including the splendid
flowers raised by I. Anderson-Henry, Esq., viz.
Henryi, Lawsoniana, and Symeiana, 10s. 6d. the set
of three plants.

CATALOGUES ON APPLICATION.

The Lawson Seed and Nursery Company
(LIMITED),
106, SOUTHWARK STREET, LONDON
AND EDINBURGH.

Charles Lawson of Edinburgh, and one of their adverts. It was this nursery which introduced the 'Lawson's Cypress'.

57

'Lawson's Cypress' — a plant
which has changed our landscape!

Facing Page: 'John Downie',
probably the best of all the fruiting
crab apples.

Malus 'John Downie'

ised by the dean of the guild. Peter's son, Charles, succeeded him in 1821, and
he also became a burgess, in 1825. Under the watchful eye of Charles Lawson,
the company expanded, and gained considerable prestige in the horticultural
world.

In 1835 they introduced the Austrian pine, *Pinus nigra austriaca*, and in 1854
they received the first consignment of seeds collected by William Murray, from the
area around the Sacramento River in California. The Horticultural Society encouraged the introduction of conifers, which was largely carried out by a group of
Scotsmen who joined together to form the Oregon Association — William Murray
was one of them. The seeds he sent back in that first consignment were *Chamaecyparis lawsoniana*, which we now commonly refer to as 'Lawson's Cypress',
and which is named after Charles Lawson.

In 1854 the firm advertised themselves as 'nurserymen, seedsmen and wood
foresters to the Queen's most excellent majesty, and to the Highland and Agricultural Society of Scotland'. They made a complete collection of all the grasses and
other vegetable products of Scotland for the Great Exhibition of 1851, for which
they were awarded a medal. The collection was subsequently divided between the
Royal Botanic Gardens, Kew, and the Highland Society Museum.

Charles Lawson became Lord Provost of Edinburgh, a position he held from
1862-5. At its peak the nursery covered over 200 acres, with seedling plants of
Rhododendron ponticum being counted by the half million. A similar number of
hollies was grown including seven acres of named varieties. In these present days
peat substitutes are avidly sought but they used a material called 'pobb' as a
substitute. It was a waste material from the ropeworks which was watered, allowed to heat, turned over and sweetened by exposure to the air — American plants
(rhododendrons, kalmias and similar plants) and other fine rooted ones thrived in
it!

Unfortunately in later years the business declined and the various nurseries
were sold off.

Another Scottish nurseryman is remembered for growing the crab apple,
Malus 'John Downie'. He had his nursery on the Corstorphine Road, about a
mile west of Edinburgh, on a site known as Beech Hill. It contained a begonia
house 80 to 90 feet long, a palm house filled with many a thousand graceful
specimens, some only a few inches high, others up to twelve feet high. Other
subjects such as gloxinias, dracaeas, cannas and caladiums each had a house of
their own. Many of these plants were used to supply their 'floral establishment' in
Princes Street, Edinburgh.

The Dawyk Estate is near the small village of Stobo, close to the banks of the
River Tweed, a few miles south-west of Peebles. The larch is said to have been
introduced to Dawyk in 1725 and silver firs were planted there as far back as
1660, about the same time that the first horse chestnut trees were planted in

Ruta 'Jackman's Blue'

Scotland, again at this estate. It is thought that the great botanist, some might say the father of plant nomenclature, Linnaeus, actually visited the estate, for he was a friend of the Naesmyth family who owned it for 200 years.

The upright growing beech, *Fagus sylvatica* 'Dawyk', which has a habit similar to a 'Lombardy Poplar', originated on the estate, which is now administered by the Royal Botanic Gardens Edinburgh.

Meanwhile, down in the fertile area around Woking in Surrey, William Jackman founded his nursery in 1810, and there were Jackmans in charge of it for the next 160 years, five different generations sharing the burdens and the joys! Originally located in St Johns, Woking, it later moved to a site of some 50-60 acres on the road from Woking to Mayford. In the 1960s it moved to Havering Farm.

Of all plants raised at Jackmans, undoubtedly the best known is *Clematis x jackmanii*. It is said that some young plants were raised in 1860, flowering for the first time in 1862, and from these plants some of our finest clematis have been developed, including that large-flowered *Clematis* 'Nelly Moser'. Other well-known plants from this nursery include *Chamaecyparis lawsoniana* 'Pembury Blue', which he obtained as a seedling from Baggesen's Nursery (they gave us *Lonicera nitida* 'Baggesen's Gold') at Pembury in Kent; and *Ruta graveolens*

Clematis x jackmanii, the plant most closely associated with this famous nursery.

Rhododendron 'Pink Pearl'

Rhododendron 'Pink Pearl' received an Award of Merit in 1897, and is still very popular today.

'Jackman's Blue', the blue rue with the pungent leaves, which George Jackman (George V, for there have been four other Georges,) found growing beside a cottage door at Ottershaw in Surrey before the second World War.

Not far away from Woking, at Bagshot, Waterers started their nursery in 1829 in an area that was famous for the growing of American plants — including kalmia, andromeda, azalea and rhododendrons. They were all acid-loving plants, and here the soil was particularly suitable for them. When Michael Waterer died in 1844 he left the Knaphill nursery to Hosea Waterer and the Bagshot nursery to John Waterer, and subsequently they started to trade separately. The name Knaphill became 'Anthony Waterer', whom we probably know better through his plant *Spiraea bumalda* 'Anthony Waterer', an excellent dwarf shrub with crimson flowers throughout the summer months. By 1860 they were exporting plants to the Continent, to India and America. By 1880 the acreage had risen to 150 acres, of which 60 acres were devoted to the cultivation of rhododendrons, one of the most popular being their *Rhododendron* 'Pink Pearl', which received an award of merit in 1897.

Later on their nursery manager, Percy Wiseman, used the Japanese *Rhododendron yakushimanum*, a very compact species, as the basis for his work which gave him the 'Dwarfs' — such cultivars as Bashful, Doc, Dopey, and Grumpy! Other introductions include *Pyracantha xwatereri*, *Prunus* 'Pink Perfection' and 'Pandora', and *Malus* 'Golden Hornet'. Anthony Waterer's home is commemorated in *Azalea* 'Homebush'.

James Arnold, a member of a famous Quaker family in the United States, left a $100,000 trust fund to the Harvard University. He had been a successful merchant in the town of New Bedford, Massachuesetts.

The opportunities that the bequest presented were quite wide, for it simply stated that it was to be used for 'the promotion of some philosophical or philanthropic purpose at the discretion of the trustees.' They chose to create an arboretum.

The initial site, covering 125 acres, was chosen for its natural surroundings — it included a brook running through a valley covered by a dense thicket of alders, a lowland swamp, a hill covered with a magnificent stand of hemlocks, and an adjoining pasture. The site is in Jamaica Plain on land which was known as Bussey Farm.

The Arnold Arboretum came into existence in 1872 and the following year the university created a chair of arboriculture. Professor Charles Sprague Sargent was the first person to hold this chair, and he also became its first director. It was a very wise choice for not only did he work hard to ensure a good design for its initial layout, but also succeeded superbly in raising money to enable them to develop a well-equipped library and a scientific garden. He also gave them his own not inconsiderable library and herbarium. Frederick L Olmsted, best known

MR. ANTHONY WATERER.

THE following interesting note is from the *Garden and Forest* about the late Mr. Anthony Waterer :—

Anthony Waterer died at Knap Hill Nurseries, at Woking, in Surrey, on November 16, after a short and painless illness, in the seventy-fifth year of his age. He is most widely known as the originator of many of the best hybrid Rhododendrons in cultivation, and he and predecessors in his family did more than any other firm to popularise the cultivation of Rhododendrons, Azaleas and other hardy shrubs of this class. The Knap Hill Nurseries, which had long been notable, grew in size and reputation under Mr. Anthony Waterer's management, and at the time of his death had become probably the greatest nursery of hardy plants of the kind. For Rhododendrons, hardy Azaleas and the choicest conifers it had no rival. Anthony Waterer had many correspondents in the United States, and his connections here date from the time of Downing, who imported plants from Knap Hill for the Capitol grounds at Washington. After Downing's death the unpaid bill for these plants was found among his papers by his executor, Henry Winthrop Sargent, of Fishkill. Mr. Sargent was a classmate of Charles Sumner, and through his assistance he succeeded in obtaining from Congress an appropriation to pay this bill. From this sprung the friendship which existed for years between Mr. Waterer and Mr. Sargent, who for many years was one of the principal horticulturists of the United States. From this friendship others sprung, until gradually all the principal cultivators of hardy trees and shrubs in the United States became friends and clients of Anthony Waterer, who of late years had devoted attention to breeding Rhodo

Top: *Metasequoia glyptostroboides* was once thought to be as dead as the dodo.

Above: Autumn colour in the Westonbirt Arboretum.

Davidia involucrata

for his work on the designing of New York's Central Park, was also involved in designing a park system for the city of Boston, and he included the Arboretum in his plans. Together with Professor Sargent he conceived the idea of combining resources with the city. The final arrangement was that the university gave the Arboretum land to the city and then leased it back from them for a $1 a year for 1,000 years, with the stipulation that the grounds would be open to the public.

Professor Sargent took cuttings from plants in his own garden to form the basis of the initial plant collection. However, the Arboretum was soon to send out its own plant collectors into Japan, China and Hawaii. It was an Englishman, Ernest Henry Wilson, who is perhaps remembered as their best collector — he brought back from China such important plant material as *Jasminum mesnyi*, *Davidia involucrata* (the handkerchief tree), *Meconopsis integrifolia* and *Thalictrum dipterocarpum*, to name but a few. From Korea he introduced *Forsythia ovata*.

Professor Sargent himself has also given us a most beautiful tree, *Prunus sargentii*, which he found in Japan.

After the death of Charles Sargent, in 1927 the Arboretum continued to play a major role in the development of plant knowledge. One major contribution arose following the visit by a Chinese botanist to the remote mountainous table-lands of the Hupeh Province. There he found a living specimen of a plant which up to that time had been known only as a fossil — and he found just three trees. In 1946 Dr E D Merrill, the director of the Arnold Arboretum, received specimens of the tree and in return sent a modest grant to Dr Cheng at Nanking. This enabled a further expedition to go back to the remote valley and collect seeds. This expedition found about 1,000 trees growing in the forests along the banks of small streams, and among rocks and boulders covered thickly by liverworts and mosses. Dr Cheng reported that without the grant from the Arnold Arboretum this second expedition would not have taken place — and we would not have *Metasequoia glyptostroboides*.

Today the grounds in Jamaica Plain cover 265 acres, a living tribute to Charles Sargent and Frederick L Olmsted.

In our own country we have a very beautiful arboretum at Westonbirt, on the edge of the Cotswolds, near to the village of Tetbury. Today it covers about 160 acres, and was the inspiration of Robert Stayner Holford, who carried out some of the original plantings in 1829. Over the years this main structure planting has been interspersed with shrub and small tree planting, all to very good effect. In more recent times this has included the planting of large groupings of a wide range of acers, particularly *Acer palmatum* and *A japonicum* types, and in the autumn these and other plantings make a superb display of autumn colours — a sight not to be missed! *Cornus alba* 'Westonbirt', a plant with brilliant crimson stems, takes its name from the arboretum.

7.
Bulbs and Corms

'Angel's Tears', named not after the angels but after Angelo.

We often think bulbs as being the glory of springtime in the garden, but there are many which can delight us during all the seasons of the year. They originated in a wide range of geographical locations and in many different soil types.

Peter Barr, born in 1825, was known as the 'Daffodil King'! He was a Scotsman, brought up as a fruiterer and seedsman in Glasgow. In 1862 he established a nursery in Tooting where he grew hellebores, irises, paeonies and bulbous plants. From his firm of Barr and Sugden, at King Street in Covent Garden, he sold bulbs, and especially daffodils. At one time he had over 500 species and varieties of daffodils in a collection of several million bulbs.

He was an extensive traveller, visiting Japan, America, New Zealand and the eastern states of Australia, as well as most parts of Europe, particularly Spain and Portugal. Patrick Synge, in his book *A Diversity of Plants* tells how Barr found the white form of *Narcissus triandrus*. It is said that he was climbing on a Spanish mountain with a guide called Angelo. Peter Barr climbed vigorously and fast, so much so that Angelo burst into tears before they reached the top. However, they found *N triandrus albus*, and ever since it has been known as 'Angel's Tears', not after the angels but after Angelo!

Peter Barr was inspired by the work of John Parkinson, who in 1629 stated that at that time there were almost one hundred different daffodils. Peter could not believe that so many had been lost in the intervening 200 years, and he set about gathering together all the variations he could find. He was successful in finding a large number and purchased two important collections, one being that of William Backhouse, a banker of Wolsingham, Durham, the other that of Edward Leeds of Manchester. Once he had got all his bulbs together he classified them according to their parentage and structural characteristics. In 1884 there was a daffodil conference, sponsored by the Royal Horticultural Society, and the classifications he had devised were generally accepted. Peter Barr was one of the original recipients of the RHS's Victoria Medal in 1897, still the society's greatest award to an individual for services to horticulture.

On the 28th March 1899 the Royal Horticultural Society's Narcissus Committee gathered for their first meeting of the new season. Mr Kendall of Newton Poppleford, Devon, exhibited 'a remarkably fine Daffodil, named "King Alfred", *a propos* of the millenary of England's greatest king.' It was unanimously granted a

Daffodil 'King Alfred'

Above: A statue of King Alfred stands in the centre of historic Winchester, where he was crowned over a thousand years ago.

Below: Daffodil 'King Alfred', named to commemorate one of England's great kings.

first class certificate. (King Alfred died on the 26th October AD 899.) The *Garden* magazine, dated the 20th May 1899, states, 'Its raiser appears to have been the late Mr Kendall, and the blooms we saw on the date came from Mr Kendall of Newton Poppleford'. The late Mr Kendall was John Kendall, a solicitor who had been born at East Budleigh in Devon but was a partner in a practice in London. He had two sons, the younger Spencer Bernard Kendall also became a solicitor and took his father's place as a partner in the practice in London, but his brother Percy John became a florist [nurserymen were often described as florists] in Newton Poppleford.

Some people in the Newton Poppleford area actually believe that Walter Hill, the Kendall's manager at the nursery, raised the special daffodil. Today in the village many fields still have daffodils growing in the hedge bottoms, a reminder of the bulb-growing days of former years. The memory of their famous flower is also kept alive by King Alfred Way, a small development of houses within the village.

The *Garden* magazine of the 1st April 1899 described the daffodil as 'a grand addition to the yellow trumpet section, and is unique in its uniform yellow tone, both of trumpet and perianth segments, and the exquisite refinement that stamps the flower as a whole. No finer yellow trumpet Daffodil has ever been shown.'

One of our less common bulbs is *Nerine bowdenii*. It is especially useful in the garden as it flowers in September-October, a period when brightly-coloured flowers are starting to become scarce. The flowers are carried on stems about two feet high, each umbel carrying about 8 to 12 of these unusual flowers with their ribbon-shaped segments of pale purplish-pink.

Nerine plants found by Mr Athelston Cornish Bowden in a remote area near King Williams Town in South Africa were sent home to his mother in Newton Abbot. This was in 1889. He also sent plants to the Royal Botanic Gardens, Kew, and Messrs Veitch's nursery at Exeter, and these flowered for the first time in October 1904. Today we know them as *Nerine bowdenii*.

A consignment of bulbs from abroad arrived at the offices of the *Gardeners' Chronicle* in June 1909. It was sent by the well-known Dutch nurseryman, Mr G C van Tubergen Jnr of Haarlem, and contained flowers of a new strain of bulbous iris, which he intended calling 'Dutch Iris'. They had been raised by crossings of *Iris xiphuim*, *I filifolia*, *I tingitana*, *I lusitanica* and others. He claimed that his varieties, whilst resembling *Iris hispanica*, flowered at least a fortnight earlier than normal Spanish Iris. One of the varieties enclosed was *I* 'Rembrandt'.

A number of years earlier another genus of plants had received similar attention, and today, as a result of this we have two very popular types of anemone. Anemone de Caen was raised by Mme Quetel of Caen, and exhibited at Cherbourg show in 1848, but received no award. By 1855 it was receiving wide acclamation, and in 1875 it was listed in the catalogue of the famous French nursery, Vilmorin.

Anemone coronia 'St Brigid' by
Wendy Walsh as prepared for
An Irish Florilegium II.

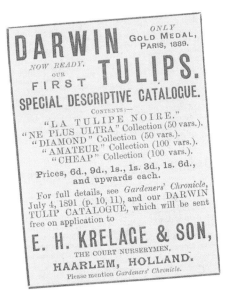

Above: Darwin tulips as advertised at the end of the nineteenth century.

Below: The unveiling of the Charles Darwin statue in Shrewsbury.

Opposite Page: Henry Eckford — one of the fathers of the modern sweet pea.

Darwin tulips

Across in Ireland, Mrs Alice Louisa Lawrenson, a gardening writer of the last century, developed a strain of semi-double anemones. She lived at Salerno, Killiney, County Dublin, later moving to Howth on Dublin Bay's rocky peninsula. We are told in the *Garden* magazine that she adopted the *nom de plume* 'St. Brigid' when she lived near the oratory of St Brigid at Nurney, Co Kildare, to avoid publicity. St. Brigid, along with Saint Patrick, is one of Ireland's patron saints.

She sowed seed of *Anemone coronaria* in the spring and gathered flowers in September. During the 1870s and early 1880s she repeatedly collected seed from only the best of her stock, gradually obtaining plants with bigger, brighter and fuller flowers. In October 1882 she sent a bunch of her poppy anemones to William Robinson of Gravetye, who was at that time editor of the *Garden,* who commented that they were very beautiful. On the 10th April 1895, Earl Cowper of Hertford exhibited flowers of 'St Brigid' at the Royal Horticultural Society's show where it received an Award of Merit.

Mrs Lawrenson is also remembered for *Narcissus* 'Lucifer' which she raised. She died in 1900 and is buried at St Fintans Church at Howth.

Tulips seem to have always had a place of special interest in horticultural circles and in October 1891, E H Krelage & Son, of Haarlem offered for sale for the first time their Darwin tulips, including 'La Tulip Noire'. They offered special collections of them — the Amateur, and Cheap, each containing 100 varieties! Earlier that year the *Gardeners' Chronicle* had revealed the story of their origin.

We are told that they were of Flemish origin, and had been produced from seed sown between the years 1860 and 1872 from the best Breeders and Broken (variegated) strains, out of the most famous collections in French Flanders. These had previously been continuously selected by one family for over a century. The collection would have been lost to horticulture had not Mr Krelage purchased it a few years earlier.

The dedication of the strain to the memory of the naturalist Charles Darwin was done with the approval of his son, Professor Francis Darwin, who wrote to Mr Krelage: 'If my father had been alive I am sure he would willingly have consented to your proposal, and I think I may safely answer for the other members of the family, who I am sure will feel pleased, as I do, at the spirit and manner in which you propose to name your new strain.'

Charles Darwin was born in Shrewsbury and a statue to his honour stands in the town.

8.
A Prima Donna among Flowers

The beginning of the twentieth century was very important for lovers of the sweet pea. They had been introduced into this country in 1700, and to celebrate the bicentenary in 1900, a major exhibition was to be held. It was through this occasion that the National Sweet Pea Society was formed.

Around this period great improvements were made to the sweet pea, and whereas Messrs Laxton and Henry Eckford can rightly claim much credit for this, nevertheless it is the name of Spencer that has been carried down through the years. This Spencer is the 'Royal Spencer' for it was from the ancestral home, the birthplace of Princess Diana at Althorp, came the waved type which became known as the 'Spencer'.

Mr Silas Cole was gardener to Earl Spencer, having followed his father in the post — between them they gave thirty-three years' continuous service. The grounds covered almost 50 acres and, of these, 14 acres were kitchen garden. We are told that Silas was not only a very capable all-round gardener, but a particularly successful exhibitor at all the leading exhibitions. It was Silas who introduced 'Countess Spencer', the first of the strain, at the first exhibition of the National Sweet Pea Society, held at the Royal Aquarium in 1901 — a particularly appropriate venue in the circumstances, for a terrific thunderstorm raged over London on that day, some of the rain finding its way through the roof. (It also brought with it some of London's soot deposit and made a terrible mess.)

However, this did not take any of the glory from the new sweet pea 'Countess Spencer', for it was awarded a first class certificate by the National Sweet Pea Society. It was described as having flowers of exceptional size and of an exquisite shade of pink.

Above & Right: Countess Spencer, and her sweet pea, the founder of the 'race' of Spencer waved sweet peas.

Opposite Page Top: Silas Cole, gardener to the Spencers at Althorp at the beginning of the twentieth century.

Some ten years later, in 1911, Mr Cole wrote to Mr Cuthbertson, of Dobbies of Edinburgh, and related the story of its birth in these words:

'With respect to the origin of "Countess Spencer", I will tell you what happened. Being always very fond of sweet peas, I turned my attention especially to them in 1898. That summer I crossed the variety Lovely with Triumph, saved the seed, and the following year, 1899, there were two or three promising seedlings, the rest being rubbish.

The good ones I crossed with Prima Donna and the next season, that was 1900, there was one plant among the seedlings much stronger than any of the other varieties. That proved to be the original "Countess Spencer". I just managed to save five seeds — one pod only. The following Spring, after sowing them, I lost three of them in one night through mice. The stock was thus reduced to two plants, but from them I saved 90 seeds. It was from these plants I exhibited at the Old Royal Aquarium for the first time. In 1902 I sowed all the seeds, every one came true, but owing to it being a wet summer, I only managed to save 3,000 seeds. 2,200 of these were sent in 1903 to America to be grown for stock by Mr Sydenham. Those that came back from America were a mixture of all sorts, no more like my true "Countess Spencer" than night is like day. It has thrown reversions; that is it has reverted to its parents, such as Lovely and Triumph, and on rare occasions to Prima Donna, but nothing else.'

Perhaps this letter highlights some of the difficulties of the early hybridist in bringing into commerce a new cultivar — something we take for granted!

Similar seedlings to 'Countess Spencer' also occurred at Mr Unwin's nursery, and he introduced the variety 'Gladys Unwin', which became the parent of many later varieties. Mr Eckford also had a similar seedling but this was never exhibited. However we still regard 'Countess Spencer' as the first of the waved sweet peas, the Spencer type.

The dwarf 'Cupid'-type sweet peas were introduced from America, having originated with Messrs C C Morse & Co at Santa Clara, California, in 1893. The first was a white-flowered miniature, distributed by Messrs W Atlee Burpee & Co, of Philadelphia. When this was first exhibited at the Royal Horticultural Society's show at Westminster on the 25th June 1895 it was the attraction of the day, and was granted an Award of Merit. However a comment in the *Garden* of the day included: 'We fail to see the value of this, which is a poor apology for a noble garden flower, and nothing will be gained by dwarfing sweet peas into comparative insignificance. The craze for a pigmy strain of our best garden flowers is to be deprecated.'

A great number of people have shown an interest in the development of sweet peas, not least the Bolton family. Robert Bolton was head gardener on a large estate near Warton, in Lancashire. As a young man he grew and hybridised pansies as a hobby, but later specialised in sweet peas. As this interest grew he

Eckford's
GIANT SWEET PEAS

Only genuine direct from WEM

Are the mammoths of the Sweet Pea World. In spite of their large size, the blooms are perfectly formed and possess an exquisite delicacy of colour not to be found in other varieties. Every grower of this charming flower should send direct for one of the following collections, which will give a long display of finest flowers of the most exquisite colours.

12 Varieties separate and named			
18	"	"	
24	"	"	5/6
30	"	"	8/-
40	"	"	10/6
50	"	"	12/6
			17/6
			22/6

POST FREE FOR CASH WITH ORDER

All the above are of the finest Exhibition quality magnificent for all purposes, containing a wonderful range of the most gorgeous colours; all strong growers, giving splendid flower-stems with giant flowers.

WRITE FOR A CATALOGUE of all the Finest Sweet Peas.

HENRY ECKFORD, F.R.H.S.,
The Sweet Pea House
(Dept, 71), WEM, Shropshire,

—

Also the finest Flower Seeds, Vegetable Seeds, Potatos, etc.

Sweet pea 'Mrs R Bolton'

spent more and more time with his sweet peas, and eventually gave in his notice to his employer so that he could devote all his time to the growing and marketing of them.

His wife, Sarah, gave him great encouragement and with the help of a small legacy they bought a house and some land at Warton Crag. At first times were hard, but by exhibiting his sweet peas at local agricultural shows, Robert began receiving requests for his seeds. In 1901 the first Robert Bolton catalogue was distributed to 'would be' customers. The beginnings were small, seeds being sorted and packed on the kitchen table, but from this a well-known and respected firm was to grow.

In 1907, Robert moved his business down to Essex. He bought some land at Birdbrook, where he found both the soil and the climate much more suitable for growing sweet pea seeds. As soon as his son, Tom, left school he joined his father in the business, for like his father he had a true love of sweet peas and was to give his whole life to their culture and improvement — so the firm became Robert Bolton & Son. The first World War brought its difficulties but they managed to keep their stocks together.

In 1923 Tom married a Lancashire girl, Marian, and brought her to Birdbrook. The years that immediately followed saw some wonderful varieties being developed, ones which were to retain their popularity for a long time.

One of these was called 'Gigantic', a beautiful white sweet pea, which reigned supreme over all newcomers. This particular variety was awarded the 'Abol' 75 Guinea Challenge Trophy for the greatest advancement since the First World War in any one species, tribe or strain of plants, and also several other awards.

The second Robert Bolton entered the company during the second World War, having started growing sweet peas when he was only five years old. As with so many other nurseries, the land had to be given over to producing food crops, but once again the precious sweet pea stocks were preserved.

Hybridising has been of great importance to the company and has brought some exciting results, one of the best varieties coming from the programme being an almond-pink flowered one named 'Mrs R Bolton', after Sarah Bolton, the founder's wife. Over forty years later it is still grown, and is still a best-selling variety.

In 1948 Robert was awarded the Victoria Medal for Horticulture for his life's work, a life that was coming to an end, for he died the following year. It was now up to Tom, and his son, Robert, to carry on the work, and that they did. Robert the third entered the company in 1975 and his sister Elizabeth became company secretary in 1976. The variety 'Liz Bolton' was named after her in 1982.

As 'Countess Spencer' appeared at Althorp Park, so Mr William Unwin produced a very similar seedling at Histon, not far from Cambridge. He named his seedling 'Gladys Unwin', which, though smaller in flower, less waved and slightly

Opposite Page Top: Sweet pea 'Mrs R Bolton'.

Opposite Page Bottom: Robert Bolton, founder of one of the companies who have given us so many beautiful flowers.

paler, had the advantage of being true to type, and became the parent of many other varieties.

W J Unwin started his business in 1903, and today, ninety years later, it is still run by members of the family.

Left: Unwins of Histon have a long involvement in the sweet pea story.

Above: Su Pollard at the Chelsea Flower Show with 'her' sweet pea.

One of our best-loved garden plants began its life in a humble workhouse garden. The 1871 census lists John Thomas Sinkins as the master of the Slough Poor Law Institution, the Eton Union Workhouse, and his wife Catherine as matron. It is believed that the well-known garden pink, with its fragrant pure-white flowers borne with great freedom above a carpet of silver-grey foliage, was raised in the 1870s by Mr Sinkins, who in turn disposed of the stock to Mr Charles Turner, Slough's famous nurseryman, who also distributed the apple 'Cox's Orange Pippin'. This was on the understanding that Charles Turner agreed to name it 'Mrs Sinkins'. It was exhibited before the Royal Horticultural Society in 1880 and received their First Class Certificate.

It was described in a nurseryman's catalogue of 1880, and Will Ingwersen writing in his small monograph *The Dianthus* stated: 'Age has put no period to her vitality, and in spite of her sins we all love her.' That statement still holds good today.

Mrs Sinkins died in 1917 and rests in the churchyard of St Marys Church in Slough; her husband lived until 1926. On the coat of arms of Slough the most prominent feature is the Buckinghamshire Swan, holding in its beak a 'Mrs Sinkins' pink.

About the time that 'Mrs Sinkins' was being exhibited before the Royal Horticultural Society, Monatgu Allwood was born at Ludford Magna in Lincolnshire, and he also was to enrich our gardens and greenhouses through his work on the same genus. His father was a farmer, but came from richer stock, whilst his mother, a Londoner, was the daughter of an architect and proud that an ancestor was one of Robin Hood's men! They had nine children, of which six were boys, and Montagu was fourth of the nine.

As a lad Montagu went away to boarding school, which he did not like, nor was he a great scholar. Even by the age of twelve he had decided that he would grow carnations for a livelihood, but not surprisingly had great difficulties in persuading others that he should do so. His parents wanted him to become a banker; when this failed they suggested he became a miller. When he attended the interview he failed to pass some simple mathematical tests, and the miller asked him, 'Do you wish to enter milling?', Montagu replied, 'No, sir, I want to be a gardener and grow carnations'.

Eventually he started work for a Mr Illman, who had a nursery at Lincoln. Montagu's father said to the nurseryman: 'Mr Illman, you give my boy an opportunity; start him at the bottom of the ladder, and if he has not sufficient brains and energy to climb up, keep him there!' Montagu made his start in horticulture at four shillings a week. By the age of seventeen he was earning twelve shillings a week, and keeping himself.

After a further two years he moved to Kent, but by the age of nineteen he and his elder brother, Edward, who was twenty years old, were discussing how they could start a business of their own. While he was in Kent he became aware of the American types of carnations, and from these he was able to develop the carnation into a commercial cut flower.

From Kent, Montagu moved to North London and found employment with one of the best growers to supply flowers to Covent Garden Market. All the time he was gathering good experience upon which to build his own company. In the same way Edward was gaining experience in the seed trade, and another brother, George, was becoming a skilled grower.

In 1910 the brothers made the break, and started the firm of Allwood Brothers at Wivelsfield Green with a capital of under £500. All three were bachelors and therefore they could cut their expenses to an absolute minimum. One of the greatest orchid growers of the period, Charlesworth, had taken an interest in the three brothers and advised them to 'start in Sussex'.

However, it was not an easy start. They had great difficulty persuading someone to lease them some land, and their first small nursery consisted mainly of four small greenhouses. Montagu had to give six months' notice to the firm he was then working with and those were most unhappy days. George had gone to America to buy some stocks of carnation plants, including perpetual-flowering carnations and malmaisons, to commence their business and nursery. The deal was only just completed in time before the plants arrived on site.

GROW CARNATIONS & ALLWOODII in your garden and greenhouse

The undermentioned Carriage Paid Collections are special value.

6 Border Carnations, distinct - 8/6
6 New Perpetual Border do. - 8/6
6 Allwodii (half pink half carnation) distinct - 5/6
ORDER ONE OF THESE COLLECTIONS TO-DAY, or write for beautifully illustrated and descriptive Catalogue of all carnations, also Cultural Guide Post Free.

Allwood Bros

The leading carnation Specialists in the World.

(Dept. 4), HAYWARD'S HEATH, SUSSEX.

Some of their early introductions were soon successes, including 'Wivelsfield White' and 'Mary Allwood'. However, soon realising that many people had no greenhouses, they decided to add hardy garden subjects to the nursery. Montagu had always dreamed of a perpetual-flowering pink, and so they decided to cross the old garden fringed white pink with the perpetual-flowering carnation which was a greenhouse plant. After many years of work the new race of plants was named *Dianthus* 'Allwoodii', by the Scientific Committee of the Royal Horticultural Society. It was an instant success and was followed by plants bred with the alpine species as parents. Also, by using *Dianthus barbatus* he produced *Dianthus* 'Sweet Wivelsfield'.

It is said that the cultivar *D allwoodii* 'Susan' was retrieved from the compost heap, and is actually named after Montagu's wife. It has a dark crimson centre surrounded by a softer pink — perhaps suggesting a black-eyed beauty!

Above Montagu Allwood, probably still the name most closely associated with carnations.

Opposite Page Top: The garden pink 'Mrs Sinkins' was raised in a workhouse garden, but today is part of a town's coat of arms; and **(bottom)** Mrs Sinkins herself.

The onion 'Ailsa Craig' was raised by Mr Murray who was head gardener at Culzean Castle at the end of the nineteenth century. Both the castle and the island of Ailsa Craig were owned by the Marquis and Marchioness of Ailsa.

10.
Food for Thought

It is easy to think that vegetables don't have interesting backgrounds, such as we've discovered with our flowers and fruits. Maybe they are not so strange or amusing, but they do have a story to tell.

In the early years of this century R H Biffen was studying the genetics of wheat, and from this early work has grown the Cambridge Plant Breeding Institute. Here plant breeding, or hybridisation, is not simply a case of recognising a 'good' plant and using that as a 'role model'; it is having a full understanding of the genes within the plant and using that knowledge to produce plants with desired characteristics.

Much of the work at the Institute, which is based in Maris Lane, Trumpington, near Cambridge, has been centred round such crops as cereals and field-grown legumes, peas and beans. However, if you go into your local supermarket you are likely to see potatoes which have been bred at this Institute — varieties such as 'Maris Peer' and 'Maris Piper'.

SELECTED BULBS · AILSA · CRAIG ·

'Majestic' potato

The Scottish Plant Breeding Station is located at Pentlandfield, Roslin, and we find both Pentland and Roslin incorporated into plant names. We have potato 'Pentland Crown', 'Pentland Dell', 'Pentland Beauty', and 'Pentland Envoy'; Rosalin has been used for potato 'Roslin Riviera'.

The National Vegetable Research Station was established at Wellesbourne, near Warwick, close to the River Avon. Many of the plants raised here have therefore been given the prefix 'Avon' — examples are lettuce 'Avondefiance', beetroot 'Avon Early', and parsnip 'Avonresister', due to its resistance to parsnip canker.

In Northern Ireland, Mr John Clarke of Ballycastle, County Antrim, has raised varieties which carry the prefix 'Ulster', including for example 'Ulster Chieftain', 'Ulster Prince', 'Ulster Glen' and 'Ulster Ranger'. However, most of these varieties of potato have now been superseded.

Changes in fashion in varietal names tell their own story. Prewar varieties had royal names such as 'Majestic', 'King Edward' and 'Duke of York'; during the war years, and in times of victory and when imperialistic tendencies were strong 'Arran Banner', 'Arran Victory' 'Ulster Chieftain' and 'Home Guard' came to prominence. In later years, from the 1960s onwards, names have taken on a more European or Mediterranean link, such as 'Estima', 'Vanessa' and 'Wilja'.

It is suggested that the name Brussels sprouts was linked with the large acreages of sprouts grown in the area around Brussels.

Similarly, the cos lettuce is thought to have originated from the Greek island of Cos where Hippocrates, the father of medicine, taught his pupils some 2,300 years ago.

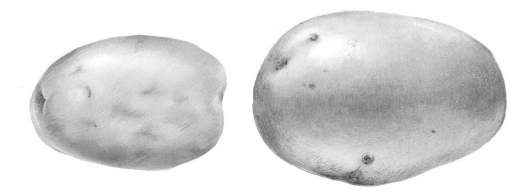

Even vegetable names have a story to tell: the Maris varieties of potato carry the name of the lane on which the research station, where they were bred, is based.

75

David Douglas. Getting us some of our most popular plants cost him his life — he died when he was only thirty-six years old.

11.
The Cost of Plant Collecting

Much has been written about some of our most famous plant collectors, but this book would be incomplete if it did not pay a tribute to the immeasurable contribution that they have made to our gardens, and also again tell the stories behind some of the plants they have given us. In many cases, whole books have been devoted to plant collectors and their works, and therefore this section will only be a 'taster' for those who would like to learn more about the people, the risks they took, and the plants they brought back.

The *Gardeners' Magazine* in 1836 devoted several pages to the life's work and death of David Douglas, a man who, although he died in his mid-thirties, gave us many of our most popular plants.

David Douglas was born in Scone, Perthshire, in 1798. He was the second of three sons, but also had three sisters. We are told he went to the parish school at Kinnoul, where he acquired 'what is usually taught there, viz., reading, writing and arithmetic'. At an early age he became an apprentice gardener at nearby Scone Palace, and is said to have been a very keen young man who also read whatever books he could borrow from his friends, often writing down extracts from them, and committing much to memory. This reading was generally confined to winter evenings, for on summer ones he went on short botanical excursions with those of a similar mind. Nearby was Perth Nursery, run by Robert and James Brown, who regularly botanised in the Highlands, and it is thought they encouraged him.

However, when he was about twenty years old he went to Valleyfield, the home of Sir Robert Preston, where there was a good collection of exotic plants and where he was allowed access to his employer's botanical library. After about eighteen months he moved on to Glasgow Botanic Gardens, where his fondness for plants encouraged W J Hooker, the professor of botany, to ask Douglas to accompany him on trips to collect material for the *Flora Scotica*. It was Hooker who later recommended Douglas to Joseph Sabine, secretary of the Horticultural Society, as a botanical collector.

In 1823 he went to America for the society, and although he returned home

Below: *Garrya elliptica*, named after the secretary of the Hudson Bay Company.

Bottom: *Ribes sanguineum*, at the time said to be in itself 'worth the cost of the tour'.

the same autumn it was only a matter of months before he was on his way again, this time sponsored by the Hudson Bay Company, to the mouth of the Columbia River, where he finally arrived at Fort Vancouver. The journey itself took eight months, but once he arrived he quickly collected vast amounts of previously unknown plant material. On board the *Mary and Anne* he had the company of John Scouler, a fellow student from Glasgow and who is commemorated in *Penstemon scouleri*. Of the several large pines Douglas discovered, he named one of the largest, *Pinus lambertiana*, in compliment of Aylmer Bourke Lambert, vice-president of the Linnaean Society. He found a specimen of this which had been blown down, and it measured 215 feet in length and 57 feet 9 inches in circumference, its cones being 16 inches long and 11 inches in circumference.

In the autumn of 1825 he entrusted a collection of seeds and plants, numbering almost 500 different sorts, to Scouler to bring back on the ship to England. In his first season he covered nearly 2,000 miles, and during his second season almost double that amount. During these travels he met Thomas Drummond (who later collected *Phlox drummondii* in Mexico) and made friends with a number of people whom we now know because of their association with a particular plant, One such example is *Garrya elliptica*, named after Nicholas Garry, the secretary of the Hudson Bay Company. The plants collected on these trips included *Cornus alba*, *Mahonia aquifolium*, *Lupinus polyphyllus*, *Clarkia elegans*, *Eschscholtzia californica*, *Pseudotsuga taxifolia* (the Douglas fir) and *Ribes sanguineum* (the flowering currant); the latter was at the time said to be worth, in itself, the cost of the tour! It was also said that so great was the number of seeds acquired that the Horticultural Society had difficulty in distributing them.

On the 31st October 1829 he again set sail for America to collect for the Horticultural Society, and also to carry out certain duties for the Colonial Office. In the spring of 1830, he landed at the mouth of the Columbia River once more. He hoped to make expeditions into the interior, where he felt his best rewards would be, but the wild state of the country and the dangerous character of the natives made this difficult. Early in 1831 he landed in San Francisco, and from there went to the Spanish settlement of Monterey where some monks befriended him. He stayed until August 1832, then left for the Sandwich Islands. From here he sent another consignment of material back to England, from which a further sixty varieties were grown in the society's garden. Among these were *Limnanthes douglasii* (the poached egg plant), *Garrya elliptica* and *Nemophila insignis*.

It was not long before he was back on the mainland, and was making his way north when he joined a cattle-party for Fort Kamloops. From there he hoped to follow the Fraser River, and then the Skeena River, making his way eventually to Siberia. However, on the Fraser River his canoe was dashed to pieces on rocks and, although he escaped with his life, all his botanical notes and collections, instruments and personal belongings were lost. Eventually he returned to Fort

The statue erected in Scone in tribute to David Douglas.

Romneya coulteri

Vancouver and, on the 18th October 1833, he left again for the Sandwich Islands.

In January he climbed Hawaii's volcanoes, Mauna Kea and Mauna Loa, went onto Honolulu and then returned to Hawaii. An account of the dreadful occurrence which took place there on the 12th July 1834 was reported in *Ke Kumu Hawaii*, a mission newspaper, and had been taken from a document addressed to the 'Britannic Majesty's Consul'.

The contents suggested that Douglas had dismissed his guide, who had warned him to beware of falling into the pits for snaring cattle. It seems that Douglas went back along the track a short distance to get a bundle he had forgotten, and as he was retracing his steps he fell into one of these pits, into which a bullock had previously fallen. He was later found dead in the pit by some natives. He was only thirty-six years old.

Without his work George Russell could not have started his breeding of the lupins, nor would our displays of summer flowering annuals be so bright. We have much to thank him for.

When David Douglas was in California he met and became friendly with Thomas Coulter, an Irishman from Dundalk, who trained at Trinity College Dublin and gained a medical degree. In 1824 Coulter left Britain to work in Mexico and spent the next ten years in that country and in California. He collected about 50,000 pressed plant specimens and also sent consignments of cacti to his botanical mentor, de Candolle in Geneva, and to his old college in Dublin. Today we remember him through that beautiful plant *Romneya coulteri* which bears solitary flowers of satin-white, delicately-textured petals which surround a mass of golden yellow stamens. Another plant which bears his name is *Pinus coulteri* which he and Douglas found in California, and which Douglas named after his friend.

I have mentioned previously gardening and botany's debt to 'men of the cloth', clergymen of many generations. I have personal reasons to be grateful, for when the Rev F Goodwin Britton died, better known as Frank to his many friends, Greta, his widow, gave me a copy of Robert Fortune's book *Three Years' Wanderings in the Northern Provinces of China*, which was published in 1847 and gives a wonderful insight into life in China at that time.

Fortune was born at Kelloe, in the parish of Edrom in Berwickshire on the 16th September 1812. Early in life he showed an interest in gardening and he became an apprentice in gardens near to his home before moving on for further training in Edinburgh, principally at the Royal Botanic Gardens. From there he moved to the gardens of the Royal Horticultural Society at Chiswick in 1842.

Although he had only been with the society a matter of months, it was Fortune whom they decided should go to China, which had just become accessible following the end of the Opium War and ceding of Hong Kong to the British. He had

WANDERINGS

IN

CHINA.

A CHINESE MARRIAGE PROCESSION.

Wanderings in China — one of Robert Fortune's books on his experiences in China.

Trachycarpus fortunei.

PLANTS AND GARDENS OF THE ENGLISH AT SHANGHAE IN CHINA.—The gardens of the English residents in Shanghae far excel those of the Chinese in the number of species of trees and shrubs they contain, and also in the neat and tasteful manner in which they are laid out and arranged. In 1845 only one or two small English houses had been built, and no gardens had been formed; but now a large English town has risen on the banks of the river, and almost every house is surrounded by a garden.

The late Mr. Hetherington was the first to attempt rearing vegetables on a large scale. He introduced Asparagus, which now succeeds admirably at Shanghae, Rhubarb, Seakale, and all the vegetables common in English gardens. He also raised the Strawberry from some seeds I sent him in 1846; but, curious enough, although it grows luxuriantly, it scarcely bears any fruit. The blossoms appear to go blind soon after they expand. I have no doubt, however, that some method will be devised to overcome this habit, and I expect to see Strawberries produced in great abundance and in perfection in Shanghae. The ground about the town is too low and wet for the growth of the Potato, and hence no one has succeeded in rearing what would be called a good crop of this desirable vegetable. In the course of time, however, when the cultivation is attempted in the higher parts of the country, we may expect to get better Potatoes here than at Macao, although the latter are usually most excellent.* Mr. Hetherington fell a victim to a fever of a very fatal kind, which prevailed in the autumn of 1848. He was a true specimen of the old English gentleman, and was deeply regretted by all who had the pleasure of knowing him.

The English Consul, Mr. Alcock, has also a good vegetable garden on the grounds attached to the consulate. There is a noble plant of the Glycine sinensis in this garden, which flowers most profusely, and becomes covered with its long legumes or pea-like fruit, which it ripens to perfection.

The two first ornamental gardens are those of Mr. Beale and the Messrs. Mackenzie. Mr. Beale's house —a fine square building of two stories—is placed in the centre of the garden. In front is a fine Grass lawn, which extends from the house to the boundary wall near the river. Behind the house there is another lawn surrounded with a dwarf ornamental wall. A wide gravel walk leading from the entrance to the back part of the garden divides the house from the business part of the premises. This garden is rich in plants indigenous to China, and also contains many which have been introduced from other parts of the world. On entering the gate the first thing which strikes a botanist is a fine specimen of the new Funebral Cypress nearly 6 feet high, and just beginning to show its beautiful weeping habit. This has been obtained from the interior, and does not grow in the neighbourhood of Shanghae. Mr. Beale intends to plant another specimen on the opposite side of the gate, and when the two grow up, a very striking and pretty effect will be produced. In the same border there are fine specimens of Weigela rosea, Forsythia viridissima, Chimonanthus, Moutans, Lagerstrœmias, Roses, &c., and nearly all the new plants sent home to the Horticultural Society from 1843 to 1846. In this part of the garden there is also a nice plant of the new Berberis japonica, lately obtained from the interior, and described in my last letter.

The American Magnolia grandiflora has been introduced here, and promises to be a very ornamental tree; its fine green leaves and noble flowers are much admired by the northern Chinese. Several plants of Cryptomeria japonica are succeeding admirably, and will soon be much more luxuriant than any the Chinese have in this part of the country. The garden has been raised with a large quantity of fresh soil considerably above the level of the surrounding ground, so that all the family of the Pines succeeds much better than in those places where they are usually planted by the Chinese; besides the latter generally spoil all their trees belonging to this family by lopping off the lower branches for firewood.

Large quantities of the Olea fragrans—the Qui Wha of the Chinese—are planted in different parts of the garden. These succeed much better here than in the south of China. In the autumn, when they are in bloom, the air is perfumed with the most delicious fragrance. Another most fragrant plant is the new Gardenia (G. Fortuniana), now common in English gardens, to which it was introduced by the Horticultural Society in 1845. In Mr. Beale's garden many of the bushes of this charming species are 10 or 12 feet in circumference, and in the season are covered with large double white flowers, as large as a white Camellia, and highly fragrant. Altogether this is a most interesting garden, and promises to be to Shanghae what the well-known one of Mr. Beale's father was to Macao.

I have made a great many inquiries about the Potato to have made its ap-

Forsythia suspensa var fortunei

no experience of overseas travel, nor of plant collecting. In the spring of 1843 he left for Hong Kong, where he arrived in July, and from there he travelled northwards until he eventually arrived at Chusan. Here Fortune saw azalea-covered mountains and rich pickings of daphnes, wistarias, wiegelas, bamboos and various other plants of interest. Whilst on that visit he also collected many chrysanthemums, tree paeonies and *Anemone japonica*, the very useful late-flowering herbaceous perennial, and sent them back to England from Hong Kong.

Again he went back to the northern region of the country, and this time visited the tea-growing district of Ningpo, a crop that was to play a very important part in his later life. Whilst there he also found a double yellow rose, which today is referred to as 'Fortune's Double Yellow', as it is not known whether it is a species or not. Unfortunately it is not hardy in this country but is said to be an ideal subject for a cold greenhouse.

In January 1845 Fortune sailed for Manilla, where he was able to collect *Phalaenopsis amabilis* which, whilst not new, was still rare in this country — it is a most beautiful orchid. One of the plants was in full bloom, and no doubt they would not have reached Britain in safety if he had not sent them in the Wardian cases newly designed by Nathaniel Ward. During that summer he was on a boat when it was attacked twice by pirates and had he not let fly with a double-barrelled gun he might have been captured. On other occasions he was robbed; once he had all his clothes taken from his cabin whilst he slept on a boat, but fortunately he slept with his money under his pillow and was able to buy some more.

Shortly after his return to England in 1846 he was appointed curator of the botanic garden of the Society of Apothecaries at Chelsea, but two years later he resigned this position to take up the opportunity of returning to China for the East India Company. His mission was to collect tea seeds and tea plants for transmission to India. He was successful in his mission, and in 1851 he arrived in Calcutta with nearly 2,000 young tea plants and 17,000 germinating seedlings. These he took to the Northern Province and laid the foundation of the Indian tea industry. Not only did he take the plants but also a team of expert tea-makers and their apparatus.

Fortune generously remembered his friends when naming his botanical finds; John Russel Reeves in *Skimmia reevesiana* and Thomas Beale in *Mahionia bealei*, although Fortune is himself remembered in *Forsythia suspensa var fortunei*, *Cephalotaxus fortunei* and *Rhododendron fortunei*, possibly the first hardy Chinese species to be introduced in this country, a parent of numerous hybrids.

Robert Fortune also collected in Japan, starting in the October of 1860, and soon discovering that the local people had a great fondness for variegated plants. As in China he was fascinated by their interest in chrysanthemums. Indeed was moved to write: 'If I can succeed in introducing these varieties into Europe they

Saxifraga fortunei.

may create as great a change among chrysanthemums as my old protégé, the modest Chusan Daisy, did when she became the parent of the present race of Pompons.'

From Japan he introduced several of their beloved variegated plants, including *Aucuba japonica*, the male form, *Kerria japonica* 'Variegata' and *Elaeagnus pungens* 'Variegata'- many of these are now popular plants in our country.

We are told he was a man of untiring industry and extreme modesty who won the esteem of all who had the pleasure of enjoying his acquaintance.

The *Gardeners' Chronicle* in its tribute to him, following his death in 1880, said: 'He is one of those whose name can never be mentioned by the gardener or the botanist without feelings of respect, admiration and gratitude.'

As stated at the beginning of our brief look at the life and collecting of Robert Fortune, not only was he an avid collector but also a prolific writer, sending regular reports, entitled 'Notes of a Traveller', to the *Gardeners' Chronicle*, and also writing many books. Let us look at how he obtained seeds of the Funeral Cypress, *Cupressus funebris*, expressed in his own words:

' . . . the most beautiful tree found in this district is a species of weeping Cypress, which I had never met with in any part of China, and which is doubtless quite new. It was during one of my daily rambles that the first specimen presented itself to my eye. About half a mile distant from where I was, I observed a noble looking Fir tree about 60 feet in height, having a stem as straight as a Norfolk Island Pine, and pendulous branches like a Weeping Willow. The branches grew at first horizontally with the main stem, then described a graceful curve upwards, and dropped again at the points. From these main branches, others, long and slender hung down towards the ground, and gave the whole tree a weeping and graceful form. It was also very symmetrical, and reminded me of some of those large and gorgeous chandeliers which one sees in large theatres and public halls in Europe.'

What could it be?

'The tree was growing in an inclosure belonging to a country inn, and was the property of the innkeeper. It was covered with a quantity of ripe seeds, a portion of which I was most anxious to secure. A wall, however, intervened between us and it. I confess I felt very much inclined to climb over it, but remembering I was acting a Chinaman, and that such a proceeding would have been very indecorous, to say the least of it, this idea was immediately given up. Another scheme was adopted with the most complete success. We walked into the inn, and seating ourselves down quietly at one of the tables, ordered dinner. When we had dined, we lighted our Chinese pipes and sauntered out into the garden, where the attraction lay, accompanied by our polite host. We led the way towards the tree, and drew his attention to it. "What a fine tree you have here; we have never seen it in the countries near the sea where we come from: pray, give us some of its

Right: *Lilium henryi.*

Below: E H Wilson, often known as 'Chinese Wilson'.

Lilium henryi

seeds." "It is a fine tree", said the man, who was evidently much pleased with our admiration of it and readily complied with our request.'

Another young man to go to China, just after Fortune's death, was Augustine Henry, but he was no plant collector. At least not at first. He, like Coulter, was an Irishman, this time from Co Derry. By training he was a medical man, although in China he worked for the imperial customs service. One of his duties was to compile a report on plants used as drugs by the Chinese. The difficulties of identifying the plants caused him to write to the director of Kew Gardens, and he offered to collect specimens for Kew. He sent them, over a period of about eight years, no less than 158,000 specimens, probably made up of about 5,000 distinct species. Of these about 500 would be new species, and amazingly about 30 new genera. Today we remember in our gardens only a few — *Acer henryi, Lilium henryi, Parthenocissus henryana, Rhododendron augustinii* and *Spiraea henryi.*

Davidia involucrata.

In 1913 he was appointed Professor of Forestry at the Royal College of Science in Dublin, forestry having been his sole pursuit since his return from China in 1900.

'Chinese' Wilson was actually born at Chipping Camden in Gloucestershire in 1876 and commenced work at Hewitt's nurseries at Solihull, near Birmingham (they are remembered by *Thalictrum dipterocarpum* 'Hewitt's Double), before going on to study at Birmingham Botanical Gardens and the Royal Botanic Gardens, Kew. It was from Kew that he was recommended to the firm of Veitch & Sons as a plant collector to work in China.

Before he set off, to prepare him for his work, he went to work at Veitch's nursery at Coombe Wood, near Kingston in Surrey. On his way to China it was arranged that he should break his journey at the Arnold Arboretum in America and meet Professor Sargent, and also learn some of the best ways of transporting plant material. He was only in Boston for five days but formed a strong friendship with Charles Sargent which was to last throughout his life.

He arrived in Hong Kong in June 1899, and after an adventurous trip to Szemao, met Augustine Henry, who told him as much as he could about the situation but particularly about where to find the one davidia tree that Henry himself had discovered. On his way to Henry he had already started his searches, and found the very beautiful *Jasminum mesnyi*, which has semi-double yellow flowers. He lived on a house-boat during the next summer and found *Davidia involucrata*, commonly known as the ghost tree or the handkerchief tree, the following April. Although this was the time of the famous 'Boxer Riots', he showed considerable courage and kept on with his work, the collecting of large quantities of seeds, bulbs and dried specimens.

Ernest Wilson returned home in 1902 but once again returned to China, again working for Veitch's, in 1903, and again with a specific commission — to obtain seeds of *Meconopsis integrifolia*, the yellow-flowered Chinese poppy. This trip was to centre on the border between China and Tibet, about 1,000 miles from his previous working area. He found the meconopsis, but also enriched our gardens with three superb primulas, *P cockburniana*, *pulverulenta* and *polyneura*, as well as two fine berberis, *B verruculosa* and *B wilsonae*, the feminine ending indicating that it commemorates his wife. These are only a few of the many treasures he collected.

His third visit to China was not funded by Veitch's, as by now the nursery was in a state of decline, but by the Arnold Arboretum. It was the opportunity for another meeting with Professor Sargent, for he called at the arboretum on his way to China, which he reached in January 1907. From this third visit we have *Thalictrum dipterocarpum*, mentioned earlier in this chapter, but also such gems as *Magnolia wilsonii*, *Hydrangea sargentiana*, *Lonicera nitida*, *Ceratostigma willmottianum*, *Rosa willmottiae* and *Corylopsis willmottianum* — the last

PLANT-COLLECTING IN CHINA.

WE learn from Messrs. Jas. Veitch & Sons that their traveller, Mr. E. H. Wilson, is about to return to this country, and in view of his remarkable success and of the importance of his introductions a slight sketch of his work may be read with interest.

The name of E. H. Wilson is now as familiar to all with any knowledge of plants as are those of Douglas, Hartweg, the brothers Lobb, John Gould Veitch, and others of the most successful collectors. He, like those named, had practically a virgin country to explore, and he made the most of the opportunity; but, unlike others, Wilson had great advantages: he had enjoyed a long special training, and the question of expense was not so serious as it was in the middle of the last century. Gifted with quite the right temperament, enthusiastic and resourceful, it is not surprising therefore that Wilson has been so successful.

Born in Birmingham, he received part of his early training in horticulture in the Botanic Gardens of that town under Mr. Latham, the ex-Curator. From Birmingham he went to the Royal Gardens, Kew, as a young gardener, and whilst there he obtained a national scholarship, which enabled him to take a course of lectures on botany at the Royal College of Science, South Kensington, under Professor Farmer. In the spring of the year 1899, Sir William T. Thiselton-Dyer, Director of the Royal Gardens, was asked to recommend to Messrs. Veitch a young man capable of undertaking a prolonged journey in China, and Wilson was suggested as a likely person.

Corydalis wilsonii.

three acknowledge the financial support of Ellen Willmott, whom I have told about earlier in the book. Wilson returned to Britain in 1909, but it was only a matter of months before he set off again, in 1910, on his final trip to China. It gave him one of his greatest discoveries, *Lilium regale*, the magnificent classic lily which grows 3 to 6 feet high and has lovely trumpets, pure white inside and purplish-pink on the outside, and richly scented. Also on this visit he found *Arundinaria murielae*, which he named after his daughter (*Rosa helenae*, which he found on the previous trip, he named after his wife) and three other liliums, *L davidii*, *L sargentiae* and *L willmottiae*.

By 1914 Wilson was on the permanent staff of the Arnold Arboretum and this time he set off, with his wife and eight year old daughter, to Japan, where he was able to do his collecting in a much more civilised manner, making use of a hotel rather than the primitive accommodation of earlier collectors. Sargent had already been to Japan and had seen something of their cherries, and now entrusted Wilson to try and find, and bring back, some of the best. It was also on this trip that he first saw the Kurume azaleas that he became strongly associated with following his 1918 visit. On that later visit Wilson was taken to the city of Kurume, on the island of Kyushu. The Kurume azaleas had been developed by Motozo Sakamoto in about 1915.

In 1919, Wilson was appointed assistant director of the Arnold Arboretum, and following Sargent's death he became the keeper. Unfortunately his life was also coming to an end, for both he and his wife were killed in a motor accident in 1930.

Another young man destined to visit China had a very different background. Reginald Farrer, the son of a political writer and enthusiastic gardener, was actually born in the year that Robert Fortune died. His home was Ingleborough Hall in the village of Clapham, in the heart of the Yorkshire Dales, not far from

AZALEA OBTUSA KURUME

(Awarded Gold Medal Mass. Horticultural Society, U.S.A., April, 1921.)

We have just received a consignment of this remarkable race of Azaleas from Japan, at great expense, by the quickest route *via* Canada. Their freedom of growth and charming colouring of its flowers will undoubtedly make these popular in every garden.

The Plants are Healthy, Bushy, and Well Branched

A LARGE COLLECTION ALSO RECEIVED OF:—

Dwarf Specimen Maples, Wistarias, Oaks, Thujas, Larch, etc., also Japanese Garden Lanterns and Water Basins

THE YOKOHAMA NURSERY CO., LTD.,
CRAVEN HOUSE, KINGSWAY, LONDON. W.C.2.

Reginald Farrer was not only a plant collector but also a botanical artist, giving us an attractive 'taste' of the local scene.

As a plant collector, Reginald Farrer also made good records of his finds in herbarium specimens. Compare this *Nomocharis basilissa* with the previous page.

Date _____ 191__

Altd. _____ feet

Locality _____

[N. "Phanig"]
N. "Basilissa"

Vern name _____

the Lancashire boundary, and also near the lower end of the Lake District. Behind the house, Ingleborough Hill rises to almost 2,400 feet, an ideal place to be brought up for someone in love with plants and climbing. Unfortunately, although he had wealthy parents, he also had a physical disability — he was born with a cleft palate and a hare-lip, which caused speech difficulties and which must have been a frustration to him. It was so bad that he never went to school, but was educated at home by private tutors. However when he grew up he went to Balliol College, Oxford, and studied for a degree.

By the age of eight he could dissect a flower expertly, and when he was four-teen he rebuilt his parents' 'rock garden', using several gardeners to help him with the heavy work. Already his eye had seen the beauty of the natural limestone formations on the surrounding hills, and he tried to recreate these as the work proceeded.

He visited the mountains of Europe with Clarence Elliott and other friends, but in 1903 he went to Japan, and recorded his impressions in *The Garden of Asia*. In 1907 he went to Ceylon to become a Buddhist. This was fully recorded in the *Times of Ceylon* newspaper at that time. In the *Gardeners' Chronicle* for 1909 there is a report that at the Royal Horticultural Society's show there was a display by the Craven Nursery, which he used at first to introduce some of our more garden-worthy native plants, such as *Geranium sanguineum subsp striatum (var lancastriense)*, *Potentilla verna* and his much-loved *Primula farinosa alba*. Later this nursery introduced some of the plants he sent back from his more distant travels.

During this period he wrote some of his best-known gardening books (although he also wrote some novels) including *My Rock Garden* in 1907, *In a Yorkshire Garden* in 1909 and *The English Rock Garden* in 1913.

His first plant-hunting expedition started in 1914 when he went with William Purdom, a most capable collector, to Kansu in China. Their collections gave our gardens such gems as *Rosa farreri*, *Buddleja alternifolia*, *Viburnum farreri* and the beautiful *Gentiana farreri*.

Farrer's second expedition was with E H M Cox to Burma, arriving at Rangoon in 1919. They had planned to go to the Tibet-Assam border, but as food and transport were not available in that uninhabited area, they chose instead to go nearer to the Burma-China border. Whilst there a party of George Forrest's native collectors came near them, which did not please Farrer, and they also had a four day visit from Frank Kingdon-Ward. This, however, they regarded as a friendly visit, and there was much talk and opening of bottles and tins. From this trip we have gained such specimens as *Primula sonchifolia*, *Jasminum farreri* and *Juniperus recurva var coxii* — the latter is known as the Chinese coffin tree, its fragrant wood being used by wealthy Chinese for their coffins.

Farrer described it as growing always at an altitude of over 10,000 feet, in a

Reginald Farrer in the robes he collected on his travels.

87

Geranium farreri

Geranium farreri — he discovered it in China in 1917.

region 'where the summer is wet and sunless, the winters of alpine cold, and the springs late, ungenial and chilly'.

At Rangoon the friends separated, as Cox had to return to England, but Farrer stayed for another season. That season was not a good one, very wet and foggy on the higher reaches. Come September he was able to rest a little, before the start of the seed harvesting season, but on the 1st October he fell ill, and on the 17th of that month he died, and was buried among those distant hills!

As a plant collector, E H M Cox wrote of him: 'He always refused to collect botanical specimens of plants because they were plants. In his estimation they had to be worthy of being translated to gardens. Thus he would skim the cream off a district and leave what might have proved to be of the greatest interest to a systematic botanist.' The *Gardeners' Chronicle* summed him up in these words: 'To friend and foe alike he was outspoken and fearless. But his words, written and spoken, made clean wounds which healed quickly. He never unnecessarily hurt a friend, and his humour and kindliness were always at hand to smooth ruffled plumes after a joust. He was a rare scholar, deeply read and widely travelled, and his sparkling conversation made him a delightful companion.'

Today he is remembered at Ingleborough Hall by a small memorial garden created by his mother, with an inscription: 'He died for love and duty in search of rare plants'. He is remembered by a wider circle of friends and followers for the

The memorial erected at Ingleborough Hall by Reginald Farrer's mother.

Opposite Page: *Primula bulleyana* — named after A K Bulley, one of the 'subscribers' to George Forrest's journeys.

books he wrote, the plant portraits he painted, and the plants that he gave us.

As the earlier collectors had been financed by horticultural societies and similar bodies, in later years they were often supported by 'subscribers', people who helped to meet the costs of the expedition and in return were given a portion of the seeds or plants. One of these sponsors was A K Bulley, whom we will meet later in our imaginary garden, and he assisted George Forrest in his collecting. Indeed, initially Forrest was recommended to Bulley by Sir Isaac Bayley Balfour of the Royal Botanic Gardens at Edinburgh.

George Forrest was born in Falkirk in 1873, and in early life worked as a chemist before going to Australia. On his return he worked as a clerk at the herbarium at the Botanic Gardens and greatly impressed Balfour.

In 1904 we find Forrest in Yunnan Province, in north-west China. To enable him to cover a wide area in detail he trained native Chinese collectors. This way many more plants were brought back and the range of material, which he and his teams collected, has become widely grown in many gardens. These include such well known plants as *Pieris forrestii*, *Gentiana sino-ornata*, *Pleione forrestii*, *Acer forrestii*, *Primula bulleyana*, *P beesiana*, *P littoniana* (now known as *P vialii*), *P forrestii* and *Mahonia lomariifolia*. *Primula bulleyana* and *P beesiana* were named in honour of his sponsor, A K Bulley and his Bees Nursery, and *P littoniana* was so called after his friend Colonel George Litton, the British consul at Tengyueh, whom he accompanied on a journey into the Mekong region and where he saw the dried plant specimens collected by the fathers at the French missionary station.

These were deeply troubled days in this region of China close to the Tibetan border, and George Forrest was extremely lucky to escape with his life. Some colleagues were murdered by the local Tibetans, but he fell and rolled deep into the jungle, and escaped. But that was not the end of it and for eight days, we are told, he was hunted like a wild animal. Eventually, having been without food for days, he arrived at a small village, just a collection of half a dozen huts, and from there he was helped by natives. They risked their own safety as he was passed along the route back to Tali-fu, where again he met Colonel Litton.

Over the years he made several trips to China, always bringing back a wealth of valuable plant material, much of it ideally suited to our British climate. In 1930 Forrest set off on his final journey before retirement, revisiting many of the places he had been before, and collecting seed in vast quantities — up to 300 pounds of cleaned seed, requiring two mules to carry it — but on the 5th January 1932 as he was preparing to leave for home he suddenly collapsed and died. He was buried next to his friend George Litton, at Tengyueh. This is not the place to record his adventures in detail, and for a fuller account I would recommend reading Alice Coats' *The Quest for Plants*.

Towards the end of his career, Forrest collected primarily for Mr J C Williams,

George Forrest — 'he sent back over 300lbs of cleaned seed'.

Gentiana sino ornata

Sorbus 'Joseph Rock'.

of Caerhays in Cornwall, and Bulley sought a new collector. This time Bayley Balfour recommended Frank Kingdon-Ward. Kingdon-Ward first went to China in 1907, to take up a post as teacher at a school in Shanghai and did not start working for Bulley until 1911. (Again Alice Coats is a useful source of information on this collector, as are copies of the *Gardeners' Chronicle* of the period.) But Kingdon-Ward was also a prolific writer, and the stories of his journeys are to be found in his books — these include *Burma's Icy Mountains*, *Return to the Irriwaddy*, *Assam Adventure*, and *Pilgrimage for Plants*. Jean Kingdon-Ward, his wife, also wrote of their travels together in her book *My Hill so Strong*, in which she recalls how they survived an earthquake, one of the greatest ever recorded. She tells not only of the fear and the noise, the landslips and the endless dust, but also of the loss of their water supply. It is through experiences such as these that men, and women, have striven to bring us the plants which daily give us so much enjoyment, and which have changed the British landscape.

To most people KW 5784 means nothing, but to those who know of Kingdon-Ward's collection registers this particular number is important for it records the

Gentiana sino ornata.

90

Meconopsis betonicifolia — the Himalayan blue poppy.

introduction into cultivation of Colonel Bailey's blue poppy, *Meconopsis betonicifolia*, a sight described by Kingdom-Ward as 'among a paradise of primulas the flowers flutter out from amongst the sea-green leaves like blue and gold butterflies'. The plant was originally discovered by Abbe J M Delavay, a French Catholic priest in 1886, and was named *M betonicifolia*, because its basal leaves resemble the betony. It was later found by Captain (later Colonel) F M Bailey during a visit through southern Tibet in 1913, and was given the name *M baileyi* by the then director of the Royal Botanic Gardens, Kew. However, seed was not introduced in this country until Kingdon-Ward and Earl Cawdor sent it back from their 1924 expedition. Following this the plant was exhibited at the Chelsea Show of 1926 by Lady Aberconway and the Hon H D McLaren, although it had previously been shown at the RHS show on the 7th April 1926 and had received an Award of Merit.

Primula florindae, which he introduced in 1924, is named after his first wife Florence, whilst *Lilium mackliniae* is named after Jean Macklin, his second wife. On one occasion in a visitors' book he described himself as being 'of no fixed abode' — a true description, for he spent his life, at least almost fifty years of it tramping the hills and valleys of China, Tibet, Assam and Burma. His death also came very suddenly, as he was discussing plans for further expeditions, at the age of seventy-three.

Our final plant hunter, Joseph Rock, was an Austrian. He was closely associated with the University of Hawaii, where he at one time held professorships in both botany and Chinese. His first trip to the great collecting grounds of Indo-China, Siam and Burma was in 1920, when he was sent to obtain seeds of the chaulmoogra tree, from which could be obtained an oil useful in the treatment of leprosy. He made a number of visits to the area over the next twenty-seven years, before finally retiring to Hawaii.

Today we remember him through such plants as *Sorbus* 'Joseph Rock' and *Paeonia suffruticosa* 'Rock's variety'. In 1926, Joseph Rock sent to the Arnold Arboretum seeds of a tree paeony which had been cultivated in the grounds of the Tibetan monastery at Choni. Professor Sargent distributed seeds of this plant to growers in various countries. However, in 1938 the monastery was burnt to the ground in a Mohammedan uprising, the monks killed and the paeonies destroyed.

Some years later the monastery was rebuilt and Rock was able to return to them seeds of 'their' paeony!

There have been many more people who, at great risk and personal cost, have brought to our gardens what is often taken for granted, and there are still those today who go in search of the unknown, the rare, the potentially useful . . . and the beautiful.

Paeonia suffruticosa — a very rare but beautiful plant.

91

CURLY
from
SHIRLEY
says . .
" WIN THE
WOOLMAN WAY "

Our Publications cover all aspects of chrysanthemum culture and are sure to help you. The new book on Indoor and Early Chrysanthemums, fully illustrated, 11/-; Chrysanthemum Culture, many coloured plates, 4/6; Monthly News Letter, sample copy 6d., 12 issues 5/-. The full catalogue for 1953-54 contains details of 1,000 varieties of **Chrysanthemums**, **Begonias** and **Dahlias** and dozens of coloured illustrations. Cultural details, stopping and timing, etc. (9d. please). Apply—

H. WOOLMAN LTD.
SHIRLEY (Dept. N) BIRMINGHAM

Chrysanthemum 'Woolman's Glory'.

12.
Famous Nurseries and the Plants They have Given (or Sold) Us

Many of the famous nurseries of this and past generations have started from very small beginnings. Some have stayed small, perhaps concentrating on a narrow range of plants, some unfortunately are no longer with us, whilst others have become large business concerns often with their own garden centres.

Henry Woolman lived in Cooksey Road, in the Small Heath district of Birmingham. By trade he was a cabinet-maker, but due to poor health and periods of unemployment life was very difficult. In 1881 he was employed by a leading firm of furniture manufacturers, his work involving him in visits to the homes of the famous to show them sketches of furniture they would, hopefully, want him to make. He was on top wages at that time — 4¼d an hour!

He was a man of many parts: a God-fearing man who never made enemies, only friends, who had an interest in astronomy, and who was an expert amateur chrysanthemum grower. He and his wife had a growing family and money was never plentiful. It was during a spell of trade depression that they hit upon the idea of turning his hobby into a way of making some much needed cash.

He already had a 12 foot by 8 foot greenhouse and he would sell his few hundred rooted chrysanthemums for a shilling a dozen post free — the advert in the *Birmingham Mail* cost thirty shillings. It would have been a blow if it had failed, but after only a few days the shillings started to pour in and it was not long before the 'Regret sold out' notices appeared. The following year they grew even more cuttings and again used the *Birmingham Mail* for an advert — it produced an even greater demand, and again orders had to be returned unfulfilled.

Another greenhouse was erected, this time for cut flowers, and this was a success. In 1885 they advertised in *Amateur Gardening* for the first time and by 1890 they had moved to larger premises, in Muntz Street, still in Small Heath. By now Woolman was concentrating full time on chrysanthemum growing, using his knowledge of chemistry and fertilizers to develop three recipes — the first for a chrysanthemum fertilizer for mixing with the soil and for top dressing, a second for watering in and a third for feeding tomato plants. He had the recipes printed, and sold them for seven pence each, post free. Over the years many thousand copies were sold.

The range of plants was expanded to include bedding plants, such as geraniums and fuchsias, and these were all delivered locally on a handcart. A customer came from Walsall and left an order for plants to the value of £10. However, they had to be delivered — Henry and his brother pushed the handcart there and back, a return journey of thirty-six miles!

It was not long before their first catalogue appeared, normal varieties being priced at 1½d each, or 1s 3d a dozen; unrooted cuttings were 1d each. New varieties cost 8d each. A further move took place, this time to Tyseley and now lobelias, asters, stocks and so on were also grown, and sold at a shilling for a box of six dozen plants. It was now very much a family business, young John being in charge of the dahlias, and his brother, Harry, the chrysanthemums. At this time the Japanese chrysanthemums were popular, and they exhibited at shows as far away as Bradford. The handcart had to make way for a pony and truck!

As further expansion became necessary, in 1907, a new site was found in outer Birmingham, at the side of the Olton Road in suburban Shirley. From there you could take a horse bus to Birmingham.

In 1913 John Woolman married Edith Victoria Smith, she being honoured in *Chrysanthemum* 'Mrs John Woolman' in 1932, and 'Edith Woolman' in 1943.

Harry was killed in a railway accident in 1926, but Henry lived until 1932, dying at the age of eighty. In 1935 John's son, John F Woolman, joined his father, and after the war he took charge of the company. His wife, Enid Goffe, is remembered in *Chrysanthemum* 'Enid Goffe', and also *C* 'Enid Woolman'. Many varieties had the prefix 'Shirley', and 'Birmingham' was a very popular late one, being grown for many years.

At the time Henry Woolman was starting his chrysanthemum business in Birmingham, Fred M Simpson was just a little lad in Otley, West Yorkshire, one of the eight children of an ironmonger who had a shop in the town.

On leaving school, Fred was apprenticed as a plumber but had to leave the trade when he contracted lead poisoning. When he was twenty-seven years old he emigrated to Canada and started a new life as a homesteader on the Red Deer River, turning a rough area into a prosperous turkey farm. Again health problems upset his plans and they returned to Otley in 1913. He continued with his interest in poultry, starting a business which developed quality strains of hens; this was on land on Pool Road, adjacent to where he later had his nursery.

In 1934, when he was fifty-four years old, Fred commenced his career in horticulture. He started with wallflowers, soon producing 250,000 each year, and about 30,000 gladioli. Again he had the desire to create something better, this time with plants.

Phlox 'Balmoral'.

Fred Simpson — nurseryman and plant raiser. He saw the potential for improvement, and achieved it.

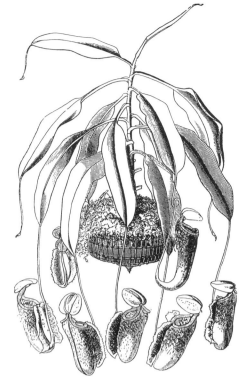

It is through nurseries such as Lemoine in France and Veitch in Devon that new plants came into cultivation and were passed on to gardeners throughout the world.

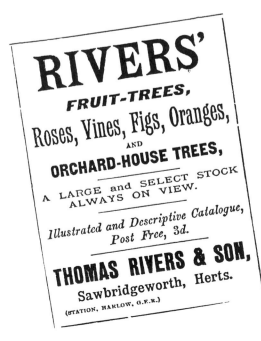

RIVERS'
FRUIT-TREES,
Roses, Vines, Figs, Oranges,
AND
ORCHARD-HOUSE TREES,
A LARGE and SELECT STOCK
ALWAYS ON VIEW.

Illustrated and Descriptive Catalogue,
Post Free, 3d.

THOMAS RIVERS & SON,
Sawbridgeworth, Herts.
(STATION, HARLOW, G.E.R.)

Phlox 'Sandringham'

It started with chrysanthemums. He was given some specimens of the Korean type from America. They were tall and straggly with a poor colour range, and were rather late-flowering for the north of England. But in them he saw the potential for improvement — they needed to be dwarfer, have a better range of flower colours and flower earlier in the season. He effected all three!

In 1938 the first three varieties were put on the market; they were named 'Lucy Simpson' after his wife, and 'Margaret Simpson' and 'Grace Simpson' after his two daughters. More and more varieties were soon appearing, increasing the kaleidoscope of colour, and these, like Russell's lupins, were distributed through Bakers' of Codsall. Their fame spread throughout the world, but it did not change Fred. He was still the same humble and friendly man 'playing about' in his small greenhouse.

He raised a *Lupin* 'Otley Yellow' and worked hard to try and produce a good yellow *Chrysanthemum maximum*, but, like everyone else so far, Fred was unsuccessful. However, his work with herbaceous phlox was far more successful, as was his Regal strain, which contains varieties such as 'Glamis', 'Windsor', 'Balmoral', 'Sandringham', 'Harewood' and 'Holyrood'.

He died in 1964, at the age of eighty-five, and it would seem his Otley Koreans have now also passed away, but his Regal phlox continue to give delight in countless gardens.

As many of our plants have their origins in distant countries, so many of our 'raised' plants have been developed in other countries of the world. One of the leading European nurseries is Messrs Victor Lemoine & Son of Nancy in France. Victor was born in 1823 at Delme, in Lorraine, the son of a gardener. He started his own nursery in 1850 in Nancy and began hybridising in 1852. Some of the early work centred around streptocarpus, but he quickly moved on, to lilacs, philadelphus, begonias and pelargoniums. In 1866 he introduced the first truly double-flowered zonal *Pelargonium* 'Gloire de Nancy', and in 1871 a double-flowered *Clematis* 'Lucie Lemoine'. The following year he again surprised the gardening world with a double-flowered plant, this time the first double-flowered tuberous begonia, *Begonia lemoinei*, soon to be followed by double-flowered *Philadelphus lemoinei*. From these spectacular developments we get such popular plants as *Philadelphus* 'Virginal' and the lilacs *Syringa x hyacinthiflora* 'Plena', *S* 'Charles Joly', *S* 'Madame Lemoine'; as well as the three cultivars which received the Award of Garden Merit in 1969 from the Royal Horticultural Society, *S* 'Katherine Havemeyer', *S* 'Madame Antoine Buchner', and S 'Mrs Edward Harding'. The nursery also introduced the well-known geranium *Pelargonium* 'Paul Crampel', and the begonia 'Gloire de la Lorraine', much loved by gardeners who had to make plant displays in large conservatories in the days of great houses and gardens employing vast numbers of gardeners.

Another good lilac, which has trusses of single deep-purple flowers up to ten inches long, is *S* 'Souvenir de Louis Spath', this name signifying its association with the German nursery of Messrs Spath of Berlin.

Coming back to our own country, we look at two nurseries unfortunately no longer with us, Messrs Rivers and Messrs Laxton.

John Rivers started his nursery at Sawbridgeworth in Hertfordshire, not far from Harlow. It is thought he was probably a gentleman's gardener. Initially the area of the nursery was limited and its range of crops wide — fruit trees and forest trees, cabbage plants, market garden produce, flowers, fruit and nosegays, and a glass of good currant wine! Indeed John's son and successor, Thomas Rivers, we are told in the magazine *Cottage Gardener*, 'actually built, for the preservation and maturation of his domestic vintage, an immense vaulted cellar, thirty feet long by ten feet wide'.

In those early days it was customary for nurserymen and seedsmen to designate their establishments with signs, and Rivers was 'The Fox'. It is said that Mr Rivers was the first in this country to cultivate standard roses for sale. He saw an old *Rosa villosa* (*R pomifera*) 'acquire the habit and magnitude of a small tree' and, as it was admired by many, he decided to train some of the same species up as standards. However, he later realised it would be easier to train up wild briars from the woods. Soon he was growing acres of roses.

In 1885 it was Mr Rivers who gave us the 'Conference' pear, the background to which is found in an earlier section. We also get from this nursery the plum 'Rivers Early Prolific'. Other important work, though of less significance today, was the production of specialist rootstocks for apples. When the East Malling Research Station started classifying rootstocks, Rivers Broadleaved Paradise Rootstock became Malling I, and the Nonsuch Paradise became Malling VI. Finally the plum 'Czar', which first fruited in 1874, was named to honour the Russian Emperor who paid a visit to this country.

Correspondence from both Rivers and Laxtons nurseries was regularly exchanged with Charles Darwin, the noted botanist, particularly on the subject of sports in plants. It was Thomas Laxton, who was born at Tinwell in Rutlandshire in 1830, who founded their nursery. Prior to starting as a nurseryman he had been a solicitor in Stamford, but had always had a keen interest in horticulture. His particular expertise lay in hybridisation and he concentrated on strawberries, apples, pears, plums, and tomatoes.

The nurseries and experimental grounds were at Bedford and at Girtford in Sandy, and there are records that he was already engaged in plant breeding by 1858. Although today most of his vegetable varieties have been superseded, some of the fruit varieties raised at Laxtons are still very popular, such as the strawberry 'Royal Sovereign', introduced in 1893; apples 'Laxton's Superb' and 'Lord Lambourne', introduced in the early 1920s; and the pear 'Laxton's Superb'.

How does one measure the contribution a particular nursery has made to our

Facing Page Bottom, and Below: Particularly in the areas of fruit and vegetables we should pay tribute to both the nurseries of Rivers in Sawbridgeworth and Laxtons of Bedford.

LAXTON'S "GRADUS."

A LARGE-PODDED FIRST EARLY PEA.

First-class Certificate from the R.H.S. after trial at Chiswick.

This is without doubt the greatest advance yet achieved in early Peas, for although the variety ripens with "WILLIAM 1ST," the pods are of the size, and as well filled, as those of "DUKE OF ALBANY," with large wrinkled Peas of the "NE PLUS ULTRA" colour when ripe; the variety being only 3 ft. in height, but very productive, and the quality quite equal to that famous Pea, as yet unvanquished for flavour. "GRADUS" is also the most distinct early Pea yet raised, and is equally good for the table and for show.

To be had in sealed ½-pint packets only, wholesale from MESSRS.

HARRISON & SONS, Seed Merchants, Leicester,
or retail from them; or from

THOMAS LAXTON, Seed Grower, BEDFORD.

Berberis darwinii

Sir Harry Veitch.

Cypripedium veitchianum.

gardens and to the wider range of plants which may be of only botanical significance? If the number of plants introduced is such a measure, then the 'House of Veitch' must be certainly Britain's premier nursery, for through their enterprise over 1,200 new plants were introduced, ranging from exotic ferns and orchids to bulbs and herbaceous plants.

John Veitch was born at Jedburgh in Scotland in 1752, but early in his working years he made the long journey down to Killerton in Devon to become land steward for Sir Thomas Acland. In 1808 he founded the Killerton nurseries at Lower Budlake, about eight miles from Exeter. These proved to be very successful, but nevertheless it was felt that there were advantages to be gained from being in the county town, so the business was moved to Mount Radford, later to be better known as the 'Exeter Nursery'.

John's son, James, was born at Killerton in 1792 and later followed into the business. James had two sons, James Veitch Junior born in 1815 and Robert Toswill Veitch born in 1823. James junior took control of the King's Road nursery in Chelsea, to which was later added nurseries at Coombe Wood and Langley, whilst Robert stayed with his father at Exeter.

Following the death of James senior in 1863, the business split into two units, the Exeter end becoming Robert Veitch & Son, whilst the London end remained James Veitch & Son. At Killerton, in 1837, there were two brothers working as gardeners on the nursery, William and Thomas Lobb. In 1840 William Lobb was sent by Veitch 'to the Brazils' as a botanical collector. His first parcel of plants sent home included *Dipladenia splendens*, and in later expeditions he sent back *Wellingtonia gigantea*. About three years later Thomas Lobb was also sent out by Veitch, in his case to Java, and he sent back two of our most beautiful orchids, *Vanda suavis* and *Phalaenopsis grandiflora*. Other plants introduced to this country because of this famous firm include such popular ones as *Abutilon vitifolium*, *Berberis darwinii*, *Desfontania spinosa*, *Escallonia macrantha*, *Hoya bella*, *Viola lutea* and *Vanda coerulea*.

James Veitch junior became an outstanding figure in horticulture, and following his death in 1869 the Royal Horticultural Society instituted the Veitch Memorial Medal, which is still awarded to 'those who have helped in the the advancement and improvement of the science and practice of horticulture' — a most appropriate citation to remind us of the one whose name it bears.

He had three sons, John Gould Veitch, Harry James Veitch and Arthur Veitch, but it was Harry, later Sir Harry, who made the major contribution in his own generation. He served the council of the Royal Horticultural Society for over twenty years, and was knighted for his work in promoting the International Exhibition of 1912, the first Chelsea Flower Show. Harry Veitch had no sons, and the business passed to his nephews, in whose hands it declined and finally closed down in 1914.

At Exeter, Robert was succeeded by his son, Peter, who travelled extensively in Australia, Fiji, Borneo and their surrounding islands, collecting many plants on the way. In 1877 he made a special journey to Mount Cook in New Zealand and collected seeds of the beautiful *Ranunculus lyallii*. From other parts of New Zealand he collected various species of *Celmisias* and *Veronicas* (now classified as *Hebe*). On his death one of his three daughters became a director of the company, but eventually the Exeter business passed into other hands.

It is interesting to note that the Veitch family came over to Scotland in the reign of Robert Bruce, and as a reward for his bravery, Gailard Veitch was given lands at Dawyck on the Tweed, which garden is featured elsewhere in connection with Dawyck Beech.

Sometimes today when we hear people talk of the good old days, it is easy to forget the hard work and sacrifices people made to try and ensure that their small business stayed alive, and perhaps even grew into a bigger one! Sir Harold Hillier told of his experiences in the early years of this century: 'I remember the days when my father, my uncle and staff worked from 6.00am to 6.00pm, finishing at 4.00pm on Saturdays, using hurricane lamps in the winter early mornings and evenings. In the days of Shroner [one of their early sites on the London road, about six miles out of Winchester] this meant a walk of 6 miles before 6.00am. Only if one was lucky was there a lift in a wagon. After a high tea, my father would work in the office at the back of 95 High Street, returning home in time for bed at 11.30pm.'

However, the Hillier story, and its plants, begins long before then. Edwin Hillier was born in 1840 and in his early years at work had gained good and wide experience in some of the leading gardens and nurseries of the day, including Veitch's nursery at Chelsea. Edwin was a good plantsman, but also an entrepreneur, and when he reached the age of twenty-four he and his wife Betsy decided it was time for them to launch out on their own.

The choice lay between purchasing a small florist and nursery business in Winchester, or acquiring a similar business in Richmond. We are told that the issue was decided on the spin of a 'trencher' — and Winchester won. To start with they had only two acres of land, primarily to produce flowers and plants for sale in the little shop, but the following year they bought a further three acres. The year 1865 was a memorable one for them in another respect: their firstborn, Edwin Lawrence Hillier, was born and they were also able to move from rented accommodation into 14 Jewry Street, which served as home, office and shop. In 1874 further land was purchased (today this site is partly used as their Winchester garden centre), and gradually the firm started to widen its activities to include providing floral displays for special events in civic and public buildings. They also widened the range of plants, and along with these sold seeds, bulbs, and even hothouse grapes and peaches to the great houses of the area. In 1877 a second son,

Above: Edward Hillier, the father of the nurseries best known for their extensive range of trees and shrubs, and the famous *Hillier's Manual of Trees and Shrubs*.

Top: *Berberis darwinii* — one of the finest shrubs from Messrs Veitch.

97

Above: *Viburnum hillierii 'Winton'.*

Top: *Thuya plicata 'Hillierii'.*

Malus 'Hillierii'

Arthur Richard, was born, and eventually young Edwin became the plantsman, and Arthur the administrative head.

The earliest record of a plant introduction from the 'House of Hillier' was *Primula sinensis flore pleno* 'Annie Hillier' in 1875 — named after one of the founders's daughters. It gained the Royal Horticultural Society's first class certificate in 1880!

Shroner, the site to which Sir Harold Hillier referred previously, contained 130 acres, and in order to purchase it Edwin had to borrow £2,000, but the loan was repaid in two years! Edwin Lawrence became very knowledgeable about conifers and in 1880 selected the form of *Thuya plicata* known as 'Hillieri'.

The Shroner Wood site was sold in 1913, about the same time that the Veitch Nurseries were broken up. Edwin Lawrence took advantage of this to acquire a wealth of choice plant material of the type sent home by such great collectors as Wilson, Forrest and Farrer.

Around this time Edwin Lawrence's son, Harold, joined the firm. He shared his father's great love of plants, in common with many people with whom he corresponded around the world. It was during the interwar period that we see more plants coming forward from Hilliers: *Malus* 'Hillieri' in 1928, *Rhododendron* 'Mrs Edwin Hillier' in 1933 and *Rosa* 'Arthur Hillier' in 1938.

At the commencement of the Second World War Hilliers had some eighty acres under cultivation. Those years had their frustration, but also their opportunities, as instanced when the Air Ministry ask them to develop techniques whereby trees of 30 to 50 feet high could be transplanted to camouflage aircraft hangars! Later, in peacetime, those techniques came to wider use in such 'instant' landscapes as the 1951 Festival of Britain site on London's south bank.

During Harold's reign the company moved forward strongly, to a state where at one time some 700 acres of land were under cultivation, and several new plants had been introduced to British gardens, including *Pieris formosa var forrestii* 'Jermyns', after Jermyns House where their eighty-five acre arboretum is today, *Viburnum x hillieri* 'Winton' which takes its name from the old name for Winchester, and *Camellia x heterophylla* 'Barbara Hillier' named in honour of Harold Hillier's wife, now Lady Hillier.

Today this internationally-famous nursery is run by Sir Harold's two sons, John and Robert Hillier. To get some idea of their standing within their profession, one must see their annual displays in the large marquee at the Chelsea Flower Show.

Left: Early days of a growing business — at 95 High Street, Winchester.

Bottom Left: *Camellia heterophylla* 'Barbara Hillier'.

Below: *Pieris formosa var forrestii* 'Jermyns'.

Carters' seeds — one of Britain's leading seed houses in the early part of the century, with large trial grounds on the outskirts of London.

The inscription from the original seed cabinet of Martin Hope Sutton.

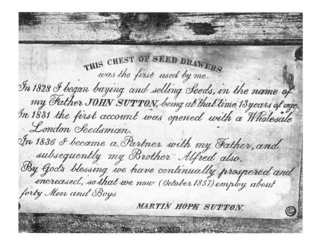

13.
Some Famous Seedsmen

For gardeners in the mid-part of this century several names quickly come to mind, notably Bees, Suttons, Thompson & Morgan, and Carters. To this I would add at least one overseas seedsman, Burpees of Philadelphia in America.

Of course the selling of seed is a very old business, but the selling of flower seeds is much more recent, although even this dates back at least to the seventeenth century.

In 1806 John Sutton began a small corn merchants' business in Reading. However, it was through his second son that the firm as we know it came into being. Martin Hope Sutton's birth was a memorable day in the family history, marked by two grave calamities — the loss of a large sum of money through the stoppage of a bank and also the failure of an extensive business with which John Sutton was connected. As an expression of faith that a bright future was in store for the son, his parents named him 'Hope', and certainly he became a blessing. He found recreation in reading botanical works and in the practical study of botany, especially in relation to flowers, grasses and foliage plants, but in these matters he received no family encouragement, indeed quite the opposite. His reading, however, naturally kindled a desire to visit famous gardens and nurseries, but as funds were limited he had to walk from one to another as part of a holiday. On one occasion, in three days, he walked from Reading to Brentford, and then through Staines to Knap Hill and Bagshot to see some new American plants, and then back to Reading, reaching it at noon, having walked twenty-one miles in the morning! Later by means of other transport he was able to visit Blenheim and Chatsworth, and even some of the famous continental gardens. Such visits inspired him to start a trial ground of his own in Reading, and the first bed of tulips in the neighbourhood became a spectacle of great interest.

In 1837 he added to the old corn factor's business the flower and vegetable seed trade, bringing his father as a partner! The company became known as 'John Sutton & Son'. A few years later his younger brother Alfred joined them and it became 'John Sutton & Sons'. They both carried on very harmoniously until they retired together on the same day in 1888.

With the coming of the penny post and the extension of the railway system, Martin saw the possibilities of pre-payment for the carriage of seed. Reading was the centre of such developments. Another innovation was the compilation of a

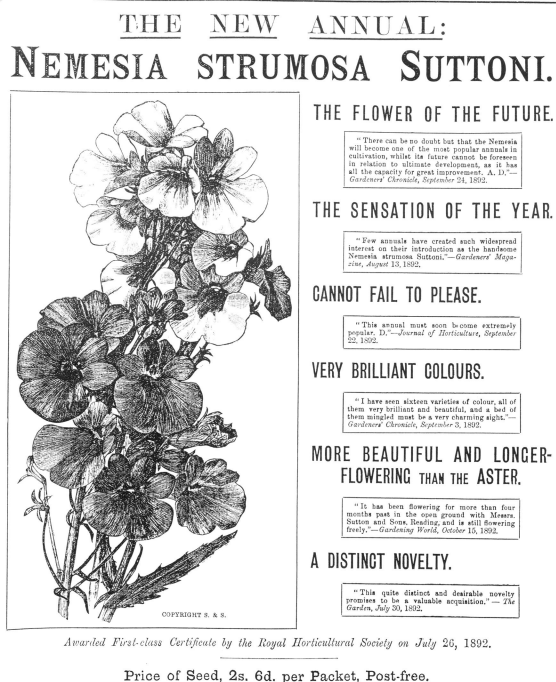

THE NEW ANNUAL:
NEMESIA STRUMOSA SUTTONI.

THE FLOWER OF THE FUTURE.

"There can be no doubt but that the Nemesia will become one of the most popular annuals in cultivation, whilst its future cannot be foreseen in relation to ultimate development, as it has all the capacity for great improvement. A. D."—*Gardeners' Chronicle, September 24, 1892.*

THE SENSATION OF THE YEAR.

"Few annuals have created such widespread interest on their introduction as the handsome Nemesia strumosa Suttoni."—*Gardeners' Magazine, August 13, 1892.*

CANNOT FAIL TO PLEASE.

"This annual must soon become extremely popular. D."—*Journal of Horticulture, September 22, 1892.*

VERY BRILLIANT COLOURS.

"I have seen sixteen varieties of colour, all of them very brilliant and beautiful, and a bed of them mingled must be a very charming sight."—*Gardeners' Chronicle, September 3, 1892.*

MORE BEAUTIFUL AND LONGER-FLOWERING THAN THE ASTER.

"It has been flowering for more than four months past in the open ground with Messrs. Sutton and Sons, Reading, and is still flowering freely."—*Gardening World, October 15, 1892.*

A DISTINCT NOVELTY.

"This quite distinct and desirable novelty promises to be a valuable acquisition." — *The Garden, July 30, 1892.*

COPYRIGHT S. & S.

Awarded First-class Certificate by the Royal Horticultural Society on July 26, 1892.

Price of Seed, 2s. 6d. per Packet, Post-free.
GENUINE ONLY DIRECT FROM
SUTTON & SONS, THE QUEEN'S SEEDSMEN, READING.

Above: Sweet pea 'Noel Sutton'.

Top: Martin Hope Sutton — 'an expression of faith'.

Left: One of Sutton's best-known introductions, but they have 'improved' many varieties of both flowers and vegetables.

101

BRIGHTEN THE BLACKOUT
planning for Greater Glories in your Garden!

Garden editors of the great national papers, the garden press generally and the Royal Horticultural Society all emphasise the great need for garden owners to contribute to the morale of the home front by keeping their gardens bright and cheerful with roses, shrubs and beautiful flowers of all kinds.

The various restrictions on travel will make your garden, next season, your most enduring pleasure and interest. For where else could you refresh your body and mind so completely and at such little cost?

Plan for colour and beauty, next season, during these black-out nights with the stimulus provided by this famous garden guide and colour catalogue. Herein lovely roses, ornamental shrubs, and border plants for garden and home decoration are portrayed in all the glories of true colour.

BEES LTD.
175D, MILL ST., LIVERPOOL

Post NOW for your Free Copy

Please send free and post paid, your

Sweet pea 'Noel Sutton'

catalogue of seeds for the amateur — soon to be known as 'Suttons' Amateurs Guide to Horticulture.' At this period many vegetable seeds grown for agricultural purposes were adulterated with dead seeds, and Martin Sutton came to the conclusion that the only way to ensure reliable seed was to have it grown under his own supervision and from his own stocks. His customers, upon seeing the resultant crops, free from any admixture of dead seed, were amazed. Customer's crops attracted the attention of their neighbours and as a result business increased at a remarkable speed.

Soon Martin Hope Sutton was called upon to attend the royal farms and also to go to the royal gardens. At that time, under the eye of the prince consort, each of the princes and princesses had their own garden plot and were taught horticulture by their father.

Martin was not only a good businessman but served the community in many ways, often anonymously. He was a man of evangelical spirit and helped in the setting up of 'Ragged schools' for the poorest in the town.

Suttons pioneered the testing of seed, being one of the first companies to have its own seed-testing laboratories. Today much of the seed is produced in Holland, France, Italy and California where agents control the quality of the crops.

The company has also played a major part in the introduction and breeding of new varieties, one of their famous specialities being *Nemesia suttonii* introduced from South Africa in 1893. Well-known varieties of sweet pea include the rich blue 'Noel Sutton' and 'Dorothy Sutton', which has rose-pink on cream flowers. In 1976 the company moved to a new base in Torquay.

The story of Bees Seeds has a completely different beginning. Arthur Kilpin Bulley was a cotton broker in Lancashire and around the turn of this century built a house, and started to develop a garden, at Mickwell Brow, Ness, on the Wirral peninsula. Indeed it was Mr Bulley's devotion to plants which led him to choose this particular site.

To enrich his plant collection he wrote to missionaries and other people stationed in various parts of the world, asking them to send him seeds of plants growing in their locality. Quite a number of people were pleased to do so and seeds soon started arriving at Ness. However, the results were not really satisfactory and Mrs Bulley has been reported as saying: 'Ness could quickly claim to possess the best international collection of dandelions to be seen anywhere'!

It soon became obvious that he needed a specialist plant collector to choose material for him, and he sought the advice of Sir Isaac Bayley Balfour, professor of botany, and keeper of the Royal Botanic Gardens, Edinburgh. George Forrest was recommended to him. At that time Forrest was a young botanical assistant at the Botanic Garden, but in 1904 he left for the Mekong/Salween region, where Tibet, China and Burma meet in the clouds.

On five separate occasions he collected for Mr Bulley, and others, but the first

Rosa 'Josephine Bruce'

two trips were funded entirely from Ness. In 1913, Bulley sponsored Frank Kingdon-Ward on the first of his many plant-collecting expeditions, and subsequently was also a supporter of Reginald Farrer, E K Balls and Clarence Elliott among others.

Arthur Bulley was quite wealthy, but he was also a socialist, and he brought some of those principles to his new initiatives. By now his gardening skills and enthusiasm had encouraged him to develop from being a private amateur gardener, into a nurseryman and seedsman. In 1905 he started A Bee & Co., but over the succeeding years it became well-known as Bees Seeds. Its first catalogue listed over 300 different saxifrages and over 100 different primulas. The catalogue for the following year, 1906, offered 4,751 varieties in penny packets.

In 1911 an extensive site at Sealand of over 600 acres was purchased for the nursery, with a head office in Liverpool. The gardens at Ness, extending to some sixty acres, were opened to the public daily, free of charge. Bulley was one of the first garden owners to do this. He also decreed that no plant should cost more that sixpence and that if anyone sought work in the gardens they were not to be turned away! The present gardens cover about twenty-two acres.

The gardens at Ness saw the introduction of many popular new plants, including *Primula bulleyana*, *P beesianum*, *Pieris forrestii* and *Gentiana sino-ornata*. The nurseries also saw the introduction of new plants through hybridisation programmes, including several roses, the best known being 'Josephine Bruce' named after the wife of a former managing director.

Arthur Kilpin Bulley died in 1942, and in 1948 Miss Lois Bulley, his daughter, gave the whole estate to the University of Liverpool with a substantial endowment. It is now their botanic garden, but many parts of it are still open to the

Opposite Page: 'Bees seeds that grow' was their motto — particularly important in wartime.

Below Left: A K Bulley at his desk.

Below Centre: A postcard produced by Bees of *Ampelopsis tricuspidata* 'Veitchi'.

Below Right: A 2d packet of Bees seeds.

2ᴰ

Bees

FRENCH MARIGOLD

Tomatoes, sweetcorn and radishes

general public, as he would have wished.

In America in 1876, W Atlee Burpee, an eighteen year old farm boy, started selling seeds as part of his farm supplies business. His mother loaned him $1,000 to start a mail order business. From this beginning, in Philadelphia, many of our garden plants were influenced and new improved varieties were quick to appear, the first being a new cabbage, 'Surehead'. Other introductions included varieties of zinnia, marigold, tomatoes and sweetcorn. In 1881 Burpee brought out an improved carrot, in 1884 a golden self-blanching celery, and in 1887 a new radish.

The company also offered a unique guarantee — if you were dissatisfied, all you had to do was to write to the company within a year about your disappointment and you would receive a full refund. By 1915 Burpees was the largest mail order company in the world, sending out more than a million catalogues a year.

Unfortunately W Atlee Burpee died that year, still a relatively young man, and he was succeeded by his eldest son David Burpee, who was only twenty-two years old. After the First World War, David became actively involved in the company and developed an intensive breeding programme to produce new flower and vegetable varieties. He was to be president of the company for fifty-five years.

Not long before his death, David Burpee related the story behind the choice of name for two of their varieties, one of which is a particularly popular plant. He said of one: 'I had been making a practice of sending advance samples, a year

After 100 years - we still guarantee*

"BURPEE SEEDS GROW"

Fordhook Farms—from an original lithograph

WHEN W. ATLEE BURPEE started selling Burpee® Seeds in Philadelphia exactly one hundred years ago, the world was a vastly different place from the one we know today. Electric lights were just beginning to appear and the first successful automobile was fifteen years in the future.

Gardens, too, were a far cry from what they are now. Most of the flowers and vegetables we take for granted were unknown in 1876. There were no hybrid corn or tomatoes, and no Zinnias or Marigolds, as we know them.

His second year in business, W. Atlee Burpee introduced a new cabbage variety he called Surehead. It was a tremendous improvement over the tough, chewy cabbages of those days,

Fordhook Bush Lima

and was an immediate success. In 1881 he brought out an improved carrot he called Long Orange, and in 1884 Golden Self-Blanching Celery. 1887 was the year of the Scarlet Button Radish. In 1894 he introduced Iceberg Lettuce, in 1902 Golden Bantam Sweet Corn, and in 1907 the Fordhook Bush Lima Bean.

That's how the Burpee Seed business grew, as gardeners all over America began to learn about the superior quality of the new varieties Burpee was introducing.

Self-Blanching Celery

Another thing they soon learned was that they could buy Burpee Seeds with complete confidence. If any Burpee Seeds did not grow to your satisfaction, all you had to do was write to the company within a year and you'd receive a full refund simply on your say-so. That's still the policy today.

By 1915 Burpee was the largest mail order seed company in the world, sending out more than a million catalogs a year. 1915 was also the year W. Atlee Burpee died, and running the Burpee Seed Company became the responsibility of his son, David Burpee, who is actively involved in Burpee's development programs to this day.

Right after World War I, David Burpee began a series of intensive breeding programs to develop new and superior vegetable varieties as well as new and better flowers. As a result of these programs, Burpee is today the leading breeder of vegetables and flowers for gardeners. Many new varieties and famous favorites are available only from Burpee.

In the 1930's the advent of hybridizing seed brought a new dimension to horticulture. Some of the results we've seen from hybridizing are truly astonishing, and some of our finest flowers and vegetables are Burpee hybrids. Burpee's Big Boy® Giant Hybrid Tomato, Ambrosia Cantaloupe, Candy Cane Zinnia, and red

Tomato

Marigold

Surehead Cabbage

and gold Marigolds are a few of the outstanding hybrids we've developed.

The science of horticulture took another giant step in the 1940's when Burpee discovered a new way to multiply the chromosome structure of flowers, and get them to burst forth in spectacular new forms. Snapdragons in particular take to this treatment like ducks to water. Another garden cinderella we've developed this way is the Gloriosa Daisy, originally the common Black-Eyed Susan that grows wild in fields.

Yes, the science of horticulture has greatly changed since W. Atlee Burpee sold his first pack of seeds in 1876.

Today we "build" new varieties of flowers and vegetables in ways that were not dreamed of a century ago.

But although many things have changed during the past hundred years—some have remained the same. In 1876, when he started the Burpee Seed Company, W. Atlee Burpee insisted that everything that carried the Burpee name would be absolutely first quality. That is as true today as it was then.

And each year we still get hundreds of letters, just as W. Atlee Burpee did, from gardeners all over the world. They come from as far away as China, India, South America, Australia, even remote Pacific islands—telling us that Burpee Seeds are growing and flourishing in those distant places. And we hope that will never change.

*After 100 years, we still guarantee Burpee Seeds grow, or you will receive a complete refund.

W. ATLEE BURPEE CO. — Quality and service since 1876

6996 Burpee Building • Warminster, Pennsylvania 18974 • Clinton, Iowa 52732 • Riverside, California 92502

French marigold 'Naughty Marietta'

ahead of the introduction of any new flower or vegetable, to a few of my friendly competitors. I had sent such a sample to Wilmer Livingstone of Ohio — it was of a new bean. Wilmer and I were having lunch together in Chicago one day when he said, "That new bean of yours certainly has a tender pod." I said, "Wilmer, I want to thank you for giving me a good name for our new bean." He said, "I never gave you a name for any new bean." And I said, "Yes you did, Wilmer, you just gave me the name Tenderpod".' Of more recent origin is the story of the naming of the French marigold 'Naughty Marietta'. David tells us: 'About February 1946, Joe Simpson, an employee of the company, and I motored south to Ormond Beach Hotel, Florida, to work on the 1947 advertising and catalogues. We needed a name for a new, single gay-looking French marigold. As we entered the hotel, the orchestra was playing the charming gay music of the musical *Naughty Marietta*. At once I said to Joe, "That's the name for our new French marigold — Naughty Marietta!".'

It was in Ipswich in Suffolk that William Thompson, a baker's son, started tending the small garden behind his father's shop in Tavern Street. Ill-health prevented him joining his father in the business, but William began to study botany. From the back garden he moved to a nursery on the edge of Ipswich, and later to a larger one. He started to publish a magazine called *The English Flower Garden,* and in 1855 produced his first catalogue, the forerunner of an unbroken line stretching through to the present time. He specialised in growing rare and unusual plants, seeds of which were sent to him from many overseas countries, and as one of the most distinguished plantsmen of his day developed friendships with such famous botanists as Sir Joseph Hooker and Charles Darwin. In 1876 *Curtis's Botanical Magazine* dedicated a volume to him — a rare honour — and twenty years later Thompson received the Victorian Medal of Honour, another high accolade. His seed business flourished and he eventually entered into partnership with John Morgan, a shrewd businessman who also offered financial resources which enabled expansion to take place.

By 1903, when William Thompson died, Thompson & Morgan had become one of the country's greatest seed firms, with a range of species and varieties far exceeding that of any of its competitors. Now John Morgan was the sole owner of the business, but in 1913 he took a partner, Joseph Sangster, so creating a family link which continues to the present day. Sangster was both a brilliant horticulturalist and a talented administrator. In 1921 he took over complete control of the company on the death of John Morgan. In about 1933 Joseph Sangster was joined by his son Murray, who had received training in horticulture in Edinburgh and at Slocock's nursery at Woking in Surrey. Today Murray's sons head the business — Keith as chairman of the British company, and Bruce as president of the United States company based in Jackson, New Jersey. The firm of Thompson & Morgan is the only British seedhouse in the USA.

Galashiels Amateur Operatic Society

PRESENTS

Naughty Marietta

1968

Above: A programme of an amateur production of *Naughty Marietta*. It was the playing of the overture in a hotel which gave David Burpee the name for his new plant.

Opposite Page Top: W Atlee Burpee, the founder of Burpees Seeds.

Opposite Page Bottom Right: French marigold 'Naughty Marietta'.

The 25th November 1939 — a new poster issued by the Ministry of Agriculture.

14.
Going for Growth

John Innes was born in London in 1829. His family was of ancient Scottish origin, and he was one of seven children. After working with an elder brother in a wine merchants business, they started dealing in property and land in the city and on the outskirts of London, and formed the City of London Real Property Co Ltd.

In 1867, John and James Innes bought a property in Merton, which was to become known as Merton Park Estate. John went to live at Manor Farm House on the estate and throughout his life he was a great supporter of the parish of Merton — of its church, its municipal affairs, its education, its caring for youth and also in the provision of allotments. As a result of this latter interest, in 1903, one of the allotment holders, a Mr Reynolds, was awarded the Knightian Silver Medal of the Royal Horticultural Society for the excellency of his allotment — an award which had not been presented for 100 years!

John Innes was passionately fond of trees. He lined the avenues of the houses he built at Merton Park with birch and plane trees, planted hollies and, wherever possible, left hedgerow oaks to grow. He also developed a model farm, where he carried out agricultural innovations and created a fine garden of his own. This has since become John Innes Park.

When he died in 1904 he left a gross estate of £338,026 — a large amount of money in those days — and of this nearly £200,000 was made available for public and charitable purposes. He left his estate and a considerable sum of money 'for the study of the growth of trees and for the improvement of horticulture by experiment and research'. The Manor Farm, together with eleven acres of land, was left for the establishment of a school of horticulture and a public park. To this was also added various residual sums which were to be used partly for the maintenance of this school.

The founding principles for the John Innes Horticultural Institute were those laid down in his will. Its first director, Professor Bateson FRS, who had previously been professor of biology at the University of Cambridge, undertook work into the causes and prevention of plant diseases, into the laws of inheritance and their application to plant breeding, and also obscure problems of plant physiology. The studies particularly included investigations into the action of chromosomes in relation to orchard crops. Other work also centred round plant chimaeras and a range of plant behaviour variations, and the working of mechanical heredity and mutations — all this was very valuable for the plant breeder, but also for the fruit grower where incompatibility between certain varieties had been a problem in orchards.

When working with plants in containers, it was found to be important to have a standard growing medium if people were to be able to evaluate results properly. They therefore set about developing a compost, or range of composts, in which most plants would grow successfully. This resulted in the introduction of the John Innes composts in 1936, long after John Innes had died! Yet this is still, for most people, the main association with the man.

The John Innes composts are still the best-known loam-based composts, consisting of loam, peat and sand to which is added set rates of fertilizers, varied according to the size and type of plant to be grown in it. A separate mixture was formulated for seed-sowing and for the rooting of cuttings. Careful notes were given as to the suitability and quality of the base ingredients, and particularly that the loam should be sterilized.

In 1939 the institution moved to Bayfordbury, in Hertfordshire, and in 1967 it moved again this time to new buildings at Colney, near Norwich, part of the University of East Anglia. Over the years the Institution has developed many plants, among them the sweetcorn 'John Innes', and *Calceolaria* 'John Innes'. Others remind us of the link with Merton, particularly the Malling Merton apple rootstocks and blackberry 'Merton Thornless'. *Streptocarpus* 'Constant Nymph', and tomatoes 'Hertford Cross' and 'Ware Cross' also originated at the Institution.

Top: John Innes.

Streptocarpus 'Constant Nymph', one of the plants raised at the John Innes Horticultural Institution.

107

Edwin Budding's machine was a development from one used to cut the nap on cloth.

HOME CORRESPONDENCE.

A MOTOR LAWN-MOWER.—I learn that one of those interesting machines, a motor-driven lawn-mower, is in use at Kew. I have not seen it, but no doubt it would interest many readers to learn how it acts there. I had the pleasure a day or two since of seeing one in use on the fine cricket ground at Bournville, Birmingham. It is one of Ransome & Sims' make, of Ipswich. The weight of the machine is considerable, some 15 cwt., but in spite of that it is manipulated with great ease, and driven with the same facility that is found in a carriage motor. I could not but admire the readiness with which the driver, who was perched on a raised seat at the back of the machine, guided it; indeed, in that respect it seemed a toy in his hands as compared with the lumbering motion of a large horse-machine. The Bournville motor has knives 42 inches in width, or rather length; behind these comes a massive roller which carries the bulk of the machine, whilst the steering power is furnished by a handwheel and a smaller roller, which follows the other. The motive power is equal to that of six horses, and can be easily utilised, doing first-rate work at the rate of six miles per hour. At that rate about an acre of lawn is cut per hour. The grass can be collected in a box, which again can be emptied easily by the driver through the action of a lever-handle. When I saw it at work the grass was being left on the ground, which, where the mower is used frequently, seems to be a ...able practice. The motive power is supplied ... cylinder, whilst a

15.
Cutting the Grass

For generations men had gone out and cut grass with a scythe, with varying results. Today the lawnmower must be the most used piece of garden equipment, and perhaps the most cursed! But how did its invention come about, and by whom?

The *Gardeners' Magazine* of 1831 gives generous space to the details of a 'Machine for cutting grass on lawns and grass-plots'. It was described not so much as an original invention, but rather as a new adaptation of one of the most efficient mechanical contrivances employed for shearing cloth, or for cutting the nap on cloth. It is likely that the inventor, Edwin Beard Budding, saw a napping machine either at the Phoenix Iron Works where John Lewis manufactured them or at Brimscombe Mills where he worked as a lad, both near to Stroud.

Unfortunately we do not know exactly when and where Budding was born, but we do know that in 1830, when he invented his lawnmower, he was living at Thrupp. Budding is a local name, and found in the parish registers of Bussage, Chalford and Bourne; indeed his daughter, Caroline, was baptised at Chalford in 1825, and his son Brice Henry Beard was born at Thrupp. We also know that Edwin died on the 25th September 1846 at Dursley aged fifty.

An agreement still exists, dated the 18th May 1830, between Edwin Budding, of Thrupp, machinist, and John Ferrabee, 'of the same place,' engineer, in which it is stated:

'Whereas the said Edwin Budding hath invented and applied a new combination of machinery for the purpose of cropping or shearing the vegetable surface of lawns, grass plots and pleasure grounds, constituting a machine which may be used with advantage instead of a sithe for that purpose; and being desirous of obtaining a Patent for his said Invention, the said Edwin Budding hath applied to and solicited the said John Ferrabee to advance the money necessary for obtaining the Letters Patent for England . . . And the said John Ferrabee having consented and yielded to the said solicitation, the parties hereto have thereupon agreed to bind themselves to observe the rules and regulations.'

Article IV stated that 'the said John Ferrabee shall have the sole control and management in every particular in regard to making, vending, using and licensing the said new machinery during the term of the said intended Letters Patent.'

In appearance the lawnmower was said to resemble a small cast iron roller, but when examined and pushed forward 'there is an obvious fitness for its object, a facility of application, a readiness and nicety of adjustment, and a workmanlike accuracy of execution, that must satisfy every mechanist'.

It was said that the cutters may require sharpening once in every two months, and that that was done by oiling the blades, and drawing the machine backwards, so that they then act like scissors, one blade upon another.

The machine was used in the Zoological Society's gardens at Regents Park, and it was operated by two men, one to draw and the other to push! It did, however, do the work of six to eight men with scythes and brooms, as not only did it mow but also brushed up the grass and lifted it into a box — all without leaving a mark! The only points to watch were that the lawn was free from any roughness or stones, and that it was perfectly dry.

The machine was manufactured by John Ferrabee's company, at the Phoenix Iron Works, as they held the patent, and was sold at from seven to ten guineas each. The writer of the article in *Gardeners' Magazine* rightly saw the development of machines which could be pulled by ponies, donkeys or small steam engines.

The early machines would not meet today's health and safety requirements. They were very heavy and had a cog-wheel drive which made it extremely noisy — 'so great was the noise caused by these cogwheel machines, that in most establishments they could not be used whilst the family was in residence before 9am., when the inmates had risen'. Later came the changeover to a watch-chain gearing and the fitting of protecting casings. Even in 1895 a contributor in the *Gardeners' Chronicle* was looking to the day when there would be 'a mower driven by electricity'. By then the steam-driven mowing machine was already in existence.

The capacity of Phoenix Iron Works must have been restrictive on growth and a licence was therefore granted to J R & A Ransome of Ipswich to manufacture

Budding wrote: 'Country gentlemen may find, in using my machine themselves, an amusing, useful and healthy exercise'.

Even the horses and ponies wore boots to avoid damaging the grass!

THE 'PATTISSON' HORSE (LAWN) BOOT

ONCE TRIED, ALWAYS USED.

Fig. 1 cannot cramp because they do not touch the Hoof.

Fig. 1.—Boot for Shod Horses.

SIMPLEST ! STRONGEST ! MOST ECONOMICAL !

Entirely Metal to Metal Fastening.

Perfect Ventilation.

USED FOR MANY YEARS IN THE ROYAL AND IN THOUSANDS OF THE PRINCIPAL GARDENS. Over 10,000 sets used in the United Kingdom.

Fig. 2.—WELTED Pattern. Copper Riveted.

SOLES of best **English Sole Leather** (Waterproofed), with Motor Tyre Rubber Studs. **Rubber Soles** strongly recommended.

The "**PATTISSON**" BOOTS can be RESOLED repeatedly equal to new ones, but this can only be satisfactorily done by us, the makers.

Fig. 2.—NO-WELT Pattern.

SILVER MEDALS Ry. HORTI. SOC., 1904, 1014. RY. INTER. HORTI. EX., 1912, & other awards.

Hundreds of Testimonials.

The Field says: "As good as anything that could be devised."

Illustrated Price List, with testimonials, from the Makers—

As no Horticultural Directories are published this year *Messrs. PATT.* are unable to make a general dist of Catalogues, but ask all [intere the upkeep of

LAWN

to write for a copy of their Price List of Specialties.

Horse Boots.
Top Dressing Distributors.
Sprinkler & Hose.

Weeding Tools.
Grass Raisers
Mowers, etc.

H. PATTISSON & CO., STREATHAM COMMON STATION, S.W.

"ADIES" LAWN EDGER
OR
AUTOMATIC SHEARS,
PATENTED.

Awarded (after trial) Banksian Medal and Certificate of Merit of the Royal Horticultural Society.

THIS INVENTION consists of **a pair of Shears,** attached to a small roller, which work automatically, and will cut the grass edges as fast as it is possible to push the machine along.

"We know not which to admire most, its simplicity or efficiency. It is as great an advance on the old Shears as the Lawn Mower was over the Scythe."
—*The Journal of Horticulture.*

OF ALL IRONMONGERS, FLORISTS & SEEDSMEN.
Price, complete, 21/-,
Or will be sent carefully packed on receipt of P.O.O. 22/- to 13, CHARTERHOUSE STREET, LONDON, E.C.

A machine obviously suitable for ladies of all classes to use!

110

Atco mowers

mowers. It is recorded that they commenced making them in 1832, which makes them the world's oldest makers of lawnmowers.

In his patent, Edwin Budding, suggested: 'Country gentlemen may find in using my machine themselves, an amusing, useful and healthy exercise.'!

In the *Gardeners' Chronicle* of 1842 a Mr W F Lindsay Carnegie of Arbroath in Scotland writes how he accidentally discovered that Budding's patent related only to England, so he got 'a very ingenious mechanic' in his neighbourhood, a Mr Shanks of Arbroath, to construct an implement for him. Mr Carnegie's lawn extended to two and a half acres, and with a twenty-seven inch machine, one man, with a small pony, was able to cut the whole area, once a week, in eight hours. From this he developed a forty-two inch machine with sufficient weight to also act as a roller, and this, again pulled by a pony, was able to cut the area in two and a half hours. Special leather shoes were manufactured for the ponies to prevent them damaging the grass!

About 1899 Ransomes saw that the internal combustion engine was the most suitable way of making lawnmowers become self-propelled, and in 1902 they produced the petrol-driven mower. The first was sold to a man in Rochester and the second to Cadburys at Bournville for their sports grounds, and both were still in service after well over half a century of regular use.

The year 1914 saw the introduction, in America, by a Mr Worthington, of what we now call the gang-mower, the linking together of a number of side-wheel mowers on a frame, making the cutting of large areas, such as golf courses, a practical proposition.

Charles Henry Pugh was born in June 1840 and spent his childhood in Newtown in Montgomery. As a young man he apparently worked as an assistant, then partner, and eventually sole proprietor of a jewellery and ironmongery business in Rotherham.

Eventually he built a factory at Rea Street in Birmingham and from there produced 'Ironmongery' for furnishing mills, particularly those in the textile industry. Charlie Pugh died in 1901 at the age of sixty — and yet our story had barely begun. He had been a man of restless energy and had adapted himself to the shifts of fashion — although he found it hard to adapt to Mr Gladstone's decision to increase income tax from 1d to 6d!

After his death the firm became a private limited liability company, with two of his sons on the board of directors, and they carried the company into the age of the cycle and motorcycle.

Immediately following the First World War there was a resourcefulness and a desire to widen their operations. It is said that a 'creation' was brought to the directors for the 'first ever' obligation-free demonstration. The chairman was enthusiastic, and although it meant going to the bank for £50,000 it was agreed to go ahead with production.

RANSOMES' AUTOMATON LAWN MOWERS.

BOX REMOVED FOR SCATTERING GRASS   **WITH BOX ON FOR COLLECTING GRASS**   **WITH SIDE ROLLERS FOR CUTTING LONG GRASS**

TEN THOUSAND IN USE, GIVING FULL SATISFACTION.—

These Machines leave no Ribs in the Grass, and are unsurpassed for keeping a Lawn or Croquet Grou
in first   They are now fitted with adjustable handles, to suit the height of the person using
Machin ... " or " plain " front rollers can be supplied at pleasure. A pair of short side rol
is sent ... front rollers when cutting long grass. The grass can be ei
collect ... Machine and left on the lawn, to prevent
grass ... steel-edged knives,
harde

No. 2.

The Golf Club Secretary

Men who appreciate
The ATCO MOTOR MOWER

The Hillsborough Golf Club.

W. FERGUSSON, Honorary Secretary.

42, CROFTON AVENUE,
SHEFFIELD. 2nd. February 1925

Dear Sirs,
In the Spring of 1921 my Committee purchased a 22" Atco Motor Mower and the Greens
Committee desire me to testify to the excellent service rendered by the machine.

For four seasons the Atco has been in
constant use, and beyond "wear and tear" re-
placements, the cost of upkeep and running
expenses have been surprisingly small.

Satisfied that the machine had justified
all that was claimed for it my Committee
purchased a 30" Atco in 1923, and after two
seasons' work without breakdown or repairs
of any kind, I unhesitatingly say that the
quality of its work is beyond praise.

Yours faithfully,

Honorary Secretary.

The above letter from the Honorary Secretary of a well-
known Club fully endorses the opinions expressed by the
Secretaries of many Golf Clubs in all parts of the country.
Let us prove ATCO claims by arranging a free demonstration
on your own grass, without obligation.

16 inch Model £50   **22 in. Model £75.**   **30 in. Model £95**
Personally Delivered and Guaranteed 12 months.
5 per cent. for cash in 7 days.

*All who take a pride in their Lawns should send for free
ATCO Booklets, "Turf Needs" and "Notes of Praise."*

CHAS. H. PUGH, Limited
Whitworth Works, 31, Tilton Road, BIRMINGHAM

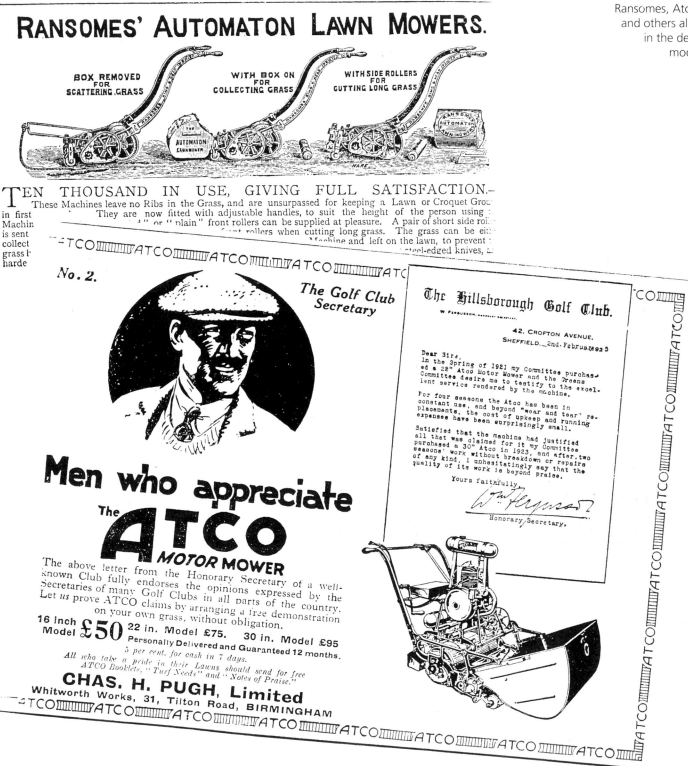

Ransomes, Atco, Greens, Lloyds and others all played their part in the development of the modern lawnmower.

MY GARDEN | AUGUST 1946

THE GRASS CUTTER

with the *SCYTHE* ACTION

The Rotoscythe is in production once again but there's a very heavy demand, so to ensure earliest possible delivery place an order *now*. The Rotoscythe works on an entirely different principle from ordinary lawn mowers — *scything* away the grass at several thousand cuts a minute and dealing equally efficiently with long grass and short.

Rotoscythe

ROTOSCYTHE WORKS, BATH ROAD WEST, SLOUGH, BUCKS.

ROTO SCYTHE

Karl Dahlman **(right)** with one of the early Flymo machines, and **(below)** the first ever Flymo.

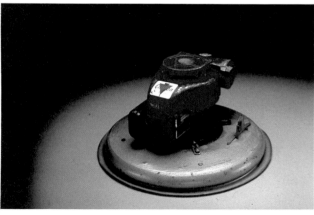

Some years earlier the company had taken into their organisation the Atlas Chain Company, and it was from these words that the letters were taken to form 'ATCO' — it was a catchy synonym, small enough to be stamped on the side plates of cycle chains, which were exported far and wide.

Prior to 1919 they had had a 'man with boy' or 'man with donkey or pony' machine, but the donkey 'died'! It was that death which lead the development department to install an engine on the old framework.

In 1921 some 900 Atcos were offered to the public, and sold. They were much lighter than comparable machines and this made transportation for servicing much easier, and in 1922 the first service branches were established, later to become a national network. In 1930 they received their first royal warrant of appointment.

The birth of the rotary mower is much more recent and took place in Australia in 1952. Mervyn Victor Richardson, a salesman for an engineering firm, put together some scrap metal, billy cart wheels, a Villiers engine, and a peach tin for a petrol tank. It was Mrs Richardson who pushed that first rotary mower against a clump of long grass and saw the grass fly away; indeed it would not only cut grass but would also cut through blackberry stems. It also had the advantage of cutting close up to trees and other obstructions.

That first rotary mower no doubt looked ugly and lacked the essential safety covers that today's mowers must have, but it was revolutionary, and in February 1953 Victa Mowers Pty Ltd opened for business. The first factory was an old shed behind a church in Mortlake in New South Wales. There was a staff of six and they produced sixty mowers a week. By 1972, when Mr Richardson died, they had produced two million mowers and by 1989 that figure had risen to five million.

Today, one of the most commonly seen lawnmowers is the Flymo, or 'the flying mower'. The hovercraft, a British invention, was the inspiration for Karl Dahlman, a Swedish lawnmower manufacturer. He became fascinated with the idea of a lawnmower which needed no wheels and could float on a cushion of air in any direction.

In this machine the drive shaft of the motor powers a fan which is attached to the cutting blades below. Air is drawn from above the cutting housing, thus creating pressure on the underside, lifting the mower from the lawn.

Dahlman's invention was exhibited at the 1963 Brussels Inventors Fair, where it won a gold medal, and received international acclaim. Britain has the largest market for lawnmowers in Western Europe and was considered the ideal location to develop and market this new concept in grass care. Today, as a consequence of this choice, Flymo are one of the worlds's leading mower manufacturers, and from their Newton Aycliffe factory they export to over sixty countries.

Today, Flymo and others continue to create new machines which aid the gardener.

113

As gardeners have needed to water plants, so they have called for suitable equipment, and thus the watering pot, and later the watering can, has been developed.

16.
Pots and Cans

It would be difficult to imagine our gardens without plant pots and watering cans.

There have been many watering cans on the market, but none so famous as those of 'Haws'. John Haws lodged a provisional specification for a 'Can fitted with a carrying handle and a tipping handle.' The complete specification stated: 'The new Invention forms a Watering Pot that is much easier to carry and tip, and at the same time being much cleaner and more adapted for use than any other put before the public.'

It was accepted on the 8th February 1886. This was a period, during the latter part of Queen Victoria's reign, when commercial nurseries were flourishing and where, in 'private service', large estates had teams of gardeners, often living in bothies, who cared for vast greenhouses and conservatories. Therefore there was a need for a good range of watering cans as watering was all done by hand.

John Haws evolved a watering can which proved to be of perfect balance, whether full, half-full or empty. It was suitable for watering plants on high shelves in the roof of the greenhouse. The design remained unchanged for a century!

John Haws died in the early years of this century and left the business to his daughters, but it was Arthur Edward Haws, John's nephew, who managed the business. He added the wire gauge baffle at the inner opening of the spout, which served to break the force of water and also stop any penetration of solid matter which might clog the 'rose' fitments. He spent much time in perfecting the design of the two standard 'roses' which were supplied with each can, one round and the other oval. The design of such 'roses' may sound straightforward, but the perforations have to be appropriately spaced and of the correct size to fit the specific size can. (Having used one for many years I know their claims to be true!)

He even went to the extent of tapering the perforations on the brass 'rose' faces by using collet-held sewing needles, with the tips ground off, for punching out the holes — he held the view that tapered holes were easier to clean when clogged with debris. Each hole was punched out separately on a foot-operated treadle by a lady worker with a special ability for this precise and exacting work. In the early days, molten lead was used to curve the rear carrying-handle, heavy gauge tin-plate was hammered by hand, and spouts and base bands

ed Watering-Pot—We have received the accompanying engraving of an improved pot from Mr. G. B. —n, 390, Oxford-street, who states that it is superior to a gen-—onsists in the roses being so formed as to give the —rown from them the nearest resemblance to a general shower of rain, which renders it peculiarly suitable for —g seedlings or other tender plants. As the brass —which connect the roses to the spout are made —tight; there is no danger of its returning outside, to —noyance of the person using it.

a, the spout to which the roses are screwed ; *b*, the box to contain either spout out of use ; *c* and *d*, the holes in which the joints are placed ; *e*, a large rose for watering flower-beds ; *f*, a smaller rose for watering plants in pots, &c.

were soldered. The cans then received two coats of paint, inside and out, before being oven-hardened.

It is said John Haws got the idea for his can whilst working in Mauritius for the colonial service. In his spare time he grew vanilla plants, but could never water them properly with the awkward can available, and so designed his own!

The company moved to Bishops Stortford in Hertfordshire in 1923. Today they are part of Haws Elliott Ltd of Smethwick in the West Midlands.

A different type of company had its birth about the time of the Great Exhibition of 1851. Richard Sankey formed his company, to make flower pots, at Bulwell near Nottingham. Richard was himself the son of a potter, his father having had a pottery at Nuneaton where he had started making 'garden pots' about 1810.

When the *Gardeners' Chronicle* visited Bulwell in 1912 the firm was making about 500,000 pots a week, in addition to pans, earthenware baskets, etcetera. The clay used was found under a thin layer of topsoil, and was dug by hand before being washed to remove any extraneous matter. It was then exposed to the effects of the weather for several months. When brought into the pottery it was watered until it had a constituency similar to putty. At that time, the pots were generally shaped by hand, although some bulb bowls were produced by machine. After being hand-shaped the pots were put on a steam-driven potter's wheel for finishing. Some of the larger pots and those for rhubarb were made in two portions which were then united together. The largest pots weighed nearly a hundredweight each before filling, and to make re-potting possible they had a false bottom over a drainage hole several inches in diameter. When it was thought necessary to re-pot a plant from such a container, the pot was lifted onto a narrow cylinder, such as a drainpipe, and the pot easily slipped down, leaving the ball of earth and roots with the plant, standing on the false bottom at the top of the column. By using this simple device it was possible to move plants out of the larger pots without either damaging the pot or damaging the plant.

After being on the wheel the pots were steam-dried, before being baked in kilns, each of which could hold 50,000 4½" pots; the baking took seventy-two hours and the process would take 12½ tons of coal! Needless to say the pottery had its own railway siding. At that time pots were shipped to such far-distant places as New Zealand, Jamaica and British Columbia and the firm was granted a Royal Warrant. The company is still in existence today.

For almost 150 years, Sankeys have been manufacturing pots of all sizes for both the amateur and professional gardener.

Haws — the professional can for many generations!

115

17.
Those Awful Latin Names!

I do not claim to be an expert on botanical nomenclature, but it is most helpful to have an understanding of the names we see on plants in garden centres or on labels in gardens such as those at the Royal Botanic Gardens at Kew or Edinburgh, or at specialist gardens like those of the Royal Horticultural Society at Wisley, in Surrey, or the Northern Horticultural Society at Harlow Carr in Harrogate.

I hope that readers will find the following limited table a starting point from which they can explore the fascinating subject of plant nomenclature. It is only when we use these names, as opposed to common names, that we can be clearly understood when we approach nurseries or deal with other plantsmen and women throughout the world — it is an international language governed by a well-designed set of rules and practice.

Firstly, the generic name: what genus does the plant belong to? *Quercus* is the generic name for what we commonly call oak, *Cheiranthus* is the generic name for the wallflower. Now let us look at a few more generic names and see, very briefly, how they originated. As will be seen the names have a Latin form and are usually derived from an ancient classical name, a native name of the country from which the plant comes, or are a commemorative name:

Aubrieta   Claude Aubriet (1668 — 1743) — a french botanical artist
Forsythia   William Forsyth (1737 — 1804) — British gardener, see page 56
Saintpaulia   Baron Walter von Saint Paul-Illaire (1860-1910) — who
               found *Saintpaulia ionantha*, the African violet
Ulex   a work used by Pliny for a type of heather
Ruta   from the Greek *ryte*, rue
Sedum   from the Latin *sedere*, to sit, describing the way some of these plants
        attach themselves to walls and roofs
Armeria   the French name *armoires*
Aucuba   from the Japanese name for the plant

Secondly, the specific epithet. Going back to our original example, together with *rubra* (red), *Quercus* forms the specific name *Quercus rubra*.

The specific epithet is also normally of Latin form and can give us some clue as to some 'specific' feature of the plant — its size, its colour, its habitat. (Occasionally there may be a sub-species and these rules similarly apply.) Whereas in the generic name the word started with a capital letter, in the specific epithet they always begin with a lower case letter:

a) The habit of the plant

altissima	very tall	*Ailanthus altissima*
ascendens	growing upwards	*Prunus subhirtella ascendens*
columnaris	column-shaped	*Carpinus betulus columnaris*
elegans	elegant	*Clarkia elegans*
excelsa	high, tall	*Picea excelsa*
fastigiata	upright-growing	*Fagus sylvatica fastigiata*
gigantea	large	*Sequoiadendron gigantea*
gracilis	graceful	*Deutzia gracilis*
grandis	large	*Abies grandis*
horizontalis	flat, spreading	*Cotoneaster horizontalis*
minor	smaller	*Vinca minor*
nana	dwarf	*Potentilla verna nana*
obtusa	blunt	*Chamaecyparis obtusa*
pendula	weeping	*Salix purpurea pendula*
prostratum	prostrate or trailing	*Lithospermum prostratum*
pumila	dwarf	*Fuchsia pumila*
pygmaea	small	*Caragana pygmaea*
repens	prostrate or trailing	*Gypsophila repens rosea*
scandens	climbing	*Senecio scandens*
suffruticosa	shrubby	*Paeonia suffruticosa* 'Rock's variety'
suspensa	hanging	*Forsythia suspensa*

b) The leaves

acerifolium	like those of Acer	*Platanus acerifolium*
acuminata	tapering to a point	*Clethra acuminata*
angustifolia	narrow	*Elaeagnus angustifolia*
aquifolium	like those of holly	*Mahonia aquifolium*
betonicifolium	like those of betony	*Meconopsis betonicifolia*
dentatus	toothed	*Ceanothus dentatus*

Below: *Trillium grandiflora flore pleno* 'Trillium' reminds us that the major part of the plant are in threes.

Bottom: *Ginkgo biloba*, ie the leaves have two lobes. The tree is one of the world's oldest living trees, fossil evidence suggesting that it has remained in an almost unchanged state

117

Hydrangea paniculata — the flowers are carried in panicles.

Flowers

dissectum	deeply cut	*Acer palmatum dissectum*
guttatum	spotted	*Erodium guttatum*
involucrata	with an involucre — a ring of bracts surrounding several flowers	*Davidia involucrata*
integrifolia	with uncut leaves	*Meconopsis integrifolia*
laciniata	torn into narrow divisions	*Rhus typhina laciniata*
lanceolata	spear-shaped	*Azara lanceolata*
laxifolius	loose, open	*Senecio laxifolius*
microphyllus	small-leaved	*Cotoneaster microphyllus*
pinifolius	like those of pine	*Penstemon pinifolius*
polyphyllus	with many leaves	*Lupinus polyphyllus*
reticulata	finely-netted	*Camellia reticulata*
rubrifolia	red leaves	*Rosa rubrifolia*
stenophylla	narrow-leafed	*Berberis stenophylla*
variegata	irregularly-coloured	*Euonymus radicans* 'Variegata'
villosa.	covered with soft hairs	*Hydrangea villosa*
xiphium	sword-like leaves	*Iris xiphium*

c) The flowers

amabilis	lovely	*Phalaenopsis amabilis*
floribunda	abundant flowers	*Malus floribunda*
globosa	spherical	*Buddleja globosa*
grandiflora	large-flowered	*Magnolia grandiflora*
hyacinthiflora	like those of hyacinth	*Syringa x hyacinthiflora* 'plena'
multiflora	many flowers	*Rosa multiflora*
nudiflorum	flowers before leaves	*Jasminum nudiflorum*
pulcherrima	pretty	*Euphorbia pulcherrima*
ornata	ornamental, showy	*Gentiana sino-ornata*
triandus	with three stamens	*Narcissus triandrus albus*
uniflorus	one-flowered	*Erigeron uniflorus*
viridiflora	with green flowers	*Tulipa viridiflora*

d) The fruits

baccata	fleshy	*Malus baccata*
cerasifera	cherry-like fruit	*Prunus cerasifera*
dipterocarpum	having two winged fruit	*Thalictrum dipterocarpum*
macrocarpa	large-fruited	*Cupressus macrocarpa*
pomifera	apple-bearing	*Malus pomifera*

e) The stems

acaulis	stemless	Gentiana acanlis
alatus	winged	Euonymus alatus
quadrangularis	with four angles	Passiflora quadrangularis
stolonifera	having stolons	Cornus stolonifera

f) Colour — flowers, stems or leaves

alba	white	Betula alba
albida	nearly white	Arabis albida
albo marginata	white margins	Hosta albo marginata
argentea	silvery-white	Achillea argentea
aurea	golden-yellow	Calluna vulgaris Aurea
azurea	sky-blue	Anchusa azurea
coccinea	scarlet	Pyracantha coccinea
chrysanthus	golden-yellow	Crocus chrysanthus
discolor	of two colours	Aquilegia discolor
glauca	blue-grey	Festuca glauca
incana	silvery-grey	Santolina incana
lacteus	milky-white	Cotoneaster lacteus
sanguineum	blood-red	Geranium sanguineum
sulphurea	light-yellow	Saxifraga sulphurea
xanthina	yellow	Rosa xanthina

Gentiana acaulis. This beautiful gentian has a specific epithet which suggests that the plant has stems which are very short, or is stemless.

Acer pseudoplatanus 'Brilliant-issimum'. The early leaves are shrimp-coloured and well deserve the description 'Brilliantissimum'.

Right: *Lysichiton americanum,* actually photographed growing wild in British Columbia, Canada.

Bottom: *Fothergilla monticola,* a lovely shrub which grows on mountains according the name *monticola.*

Below: *Ruta graveolens —* *graveolens* means heavily-scented, some people might say smelly!

g) Scents

fragrans	fragrant	*Osmanthus fragrans*
graveolens	heavily scented	*Ruta graveolens*
odora	fragrant	*Daphne odora*

h) Habitat

alpinus	alpine	*Aster alpinus*
aquatica	growing in or near water	*Gleditsia aquatica*
calcarea	lime	*Polygala calcarea*
maritima	sea	*Armeria maritima*
montanum	mountains	*Teucrium montanum*
palustris	marsh loving	*Caltha palustris*
rupestris	rock loving	*Veronica rupestris*
sylvatica	in woods	*Fagus sylvatica*

i) Geographical

australis	southern	*Erica australis*
californica	from California	*Zauschneria californica*
canadensis	from Canada	*Rubus canadensis*
caucasica	from the Caucasus	*Scabiosa caucasica*
garganica	from Mount Gargano (in southern Italy)	*Campanula garganica*
japonica	from Japan	*Mahonia japonica*
nepalensis	from Nepal	*Potentilla nepalensis*
nootkatensis	from Nootka Sound, British Columbia	*Chamaecyparis nootkatensis*
sinensis	from China	*Wisteria sinensis*

j) After plant collectors, their sponsors and friends

beesiana	Bees nursery	*Primula beesiana*
bulleyana	A K Bulley (owner of Bees)	*Primula bulleyana*
coulteri	after Thomas Coulter	*Romneya coulteri*
davidia	after Abbe Armand David	*Davidia involucrata*
farreri	after Reginald Farrer	*Potentilla farreri*
florindae	after Florence, Kingdom-Ward's first wife	*Primula florindae*
mackliniae	after Jean Macklin, Kingdom-Ward's second wife	*Lilium mackliniae*
veitchii	after James Veitch who had his nursery at Exeter	*Spiraea veitchii*
willmottiae	after Ellen Willmott	*Ceratostigma willmottianum*
wilsonii	after E H Wilson	*Magnolia wilsonii*
wilsoniae	after E H Wilson's wife	*Berberis wilsoniae*

k) Miscellaneous origins

funebris	funereal, belonging to graveyards	*Cupressus funebris*
insigne	distinguished	*Rhododendron insigne*
pulverulenta	powdered with dust	*Primula pulverulenta*
vulgaris	common	*Calluna vulgaris*

Bottom: *Lilium regale* — a beautiful flower, *regale* meaning 'of outstanding merit'.

Below: *Hypericum forrestii*. George Forrest was a famous Scottish plant-collector and several plants carry his name.

This list is not intended to be a comprehensive guide to where information on the backgrounds to our plants can be found, but is rather a starting point for those who would wish to pursue the matter further. Other reference points are old catalogues, celebration booklets produced by companies and archive material contained in libraries and museums.

Because a book is mentioned here it does not indicate that it has been used by me for textual or illustrative material.

Magazines and journals consulted include:

Gardeners' Chronicle
The *Garden*
Journal of the Royal Horticultural Society
Journal of Horticulture & Cottage Gardener
The *Gardeners' Magazine*

Related books and ones helpful to this study area include:

The Early Horticulturists, Ronald Webber (David & Charles 1968)
Traveller in a Vanished Landscape, William Morwood (Gentry Books 1973)
Trees & Shrubs Hardy in the British Isles, W J Bean (John Murray)
Hillier's Manual of Trees and Shrubs, Hilliers (David & Charles)
A Gardeners' Dictionary of Plant Names, William T Stearn (Cassell 1972)
The Story of the Royal Horticultural Society, H R Fletcher (Oxford 1969)
The Quest for Plants, Alice M Coats (Studio Vista 1969)
The Makers of Heavenly Roses, Jack Harkness (Dent 1978)
Who does your Garden Grow, Alex Pankhurst (Earls Eye Publishing 1992)
The Plant Finder, Chris Philip (MPC)
The New Royal Horticultural Society Dictionary of Gardening, Royal
    Horticultural Society (Macmillan 1992)
The Coming of the Flowers, A W Anderson (Williams & Norgate)
Irish Florilegium II, E Charles Nelson and Wendy Walsh (Thames & Hudson 1992)
Horticultural Who's Who, Simmonds (1948)
A Rose Odyssey, J H Nicolas (Doubleday, Doran & Co 1937)